CULTURES OF THE WORLD
Slovenia

Cavendish
Square

New York

Published in 2021 by Cavendish Square Publishing, LLC
243 5th Avenue, Suite 136, New York, NY 10016

Library of Congress Cataloging-in-Publication Data

Names: Gottfried, Ted, author. | Nevins, Debbie, author.
Title: Slovenia / Ted Gottfried, Debbie Nevins.
Description: Third edition. | New York, NY : Cavendish Square Publishing,
  2021. | Series: Cultures of the world | Includes bibliographical
  references and index.
Identifiers: LCCN 2019055641 (print) | LCCN 2019055642 (ebook) | ISBN
  9781502655950 (library binding) | ISBN 9781502655967 (ebook)
Subjects: LCSH: Slovenia--Juvenile literature.
Classification: LCC DR1360 .G678 2021 (print) | LCC DR1360 (ebook) | DDC
  949.73--dc23
LC record available at https://lccn.loc.gov/2019055641
LC ebook record available at https://lccn.loc.gov/2019055642

Editor, third edition: Debbie Nevins
Designer, third edition: Jessica Nevins

The photographs in this book are used with the permission of: Cover Mlenny/iStock/Getty Images Plus; p.1 Valentin Valkov/Shutterstock.com; p. 3 JGA/Shutterstock.com; pp. 5, 77, 99 B7 Photography/Shutterstock.com; pp. 6, 12 Peter Hermes Furian/Shutterstock.com; pp. 7, 64 Natalia Deriabina/Shutterstock.com; p. 8 Goran Jakus/Shutterstock.com; p. 10 kamnacestach/Shutterstock.com; p. 13 Olesya Baron/Shutterstock.com; p. 14 Sopotnicki/Shutterstock.com; p. 15, 53, 106 Andrej Safaric/Shutterstock.com; pp. 16, 44, 58, 66, 80, 115 Matej Kastelic/Shutterstock.com; p. 17 hbpro/Shutterstock.com; p. 18 vvvita/Shutterstock.com; p. 19 marcin jucha/Shutterstock.com; pp. 20, 98 Roman Babakin/Shutterstock.com; p. 21 sn0wball1/Shutterstock.com; p. 22 Vladuska/Shutterstock.com; p. 24 Ekaterina McClaud/Shutterstock.com; p. 25 Pavel Dobrovsky/Shutterstock.com; p. 26 goodcat/Shutterstock.com; p. 28 Keystone/Hulton Archive/Getty Images; p. 30 Jacques Langevin/Sygma/Sygma via Getty Images; pp. 32, 60, 69 Jure Makovec/AFP via Getty Images; pp. 34, 37 Alexandros Michailidis/Shutterstock.com; p. 40 joachim affeldt/Shutterstock.com; p. 43 jean-francois me/Shutterstock.com; p. 45 Bodo Photography/Shutterstock.com; p. 48 Marieke Kramer/Shutterstock.com; p. 50 imarovich/Shutterstock.com; p. 51 bellena/Shutterstock.com; p. 52 Xseon/Shutterstock.com; p. 54 Clari Massimiliano/Shutterstock.com; p. 55 blazg/Shutterstock.com; p. 56 Neja Hrovat/Shutterstock.com; pp. 61, 100, 110 Maljalen/Shutterstock.com; p. 62 Frederic Legrand - COMEO/Shutterstock.com; p. 68 Telly/Shutterstock.com; p. 72 Nosova Elizaveta/Shutterstock.com; pp. 74, 78 milosk50/Shutterstock.com; p. 75 S-F/Shutterstock.com; p. 79 Littleaom/Shutterstock.com; pp. 82, 97 TMP_An_Instant_of_Time/Shutterstock.com; p. 85 Adriana Iacob/Shutterstock.com; p. 86 http://nl.ijs.si/e-zrc/bs/html/bsFC.html/Wikimedia Commons/File:Brižinski spomeniki 3.png/PD-old; p. 88 bumihills; pp. 90, 125 Veronika Kovalenko/Shutterstock.com; p. 91 Naeblys/iStock Editorial/Getty Images Plus; p. 92 kavcicm/Shutterstock.com; p. 93 Mattis Kaminer/Shutterstock.com; p. 95 Anton Cebej/Wikimedia Commons/File:Anton Cebej - Sv. Leopold.jpg/CC-PD-Mark; p. 96 dalbera from Paris, France/Wikimedia Commons/File:Flûte paléolithique (musée national de Slovénie, Ljubljana) (9420310527).jpg/CC BY 2.0; p. 102 Mountain Cubs/Shutterstock.com; p. 104 Mikadun/Shutterstock.com; p. 105 A_Mikhail/Shutterstock.com; p. 107 BoPhotoAdventures/Shutterstock.com; pp. 108 Gints Ivuskans/Shutterstock.com; p. 112 Xseon/Shutterstock.com; p. 114 TTL media/Shutterstock.com; p. 117 dejan_k/Shutterstock.com; p. 118 s5iztok/iStock/Getty Images Plus; p. 120 pcruciatti/Shutterstock.com; p. 122 Jelena990/Shutterstock.com; p. 123 JRP Studio/Shutterstock.com; p. 124 Visionsi/Shutterstock.com; p. 126 Filip Koric/Shutterstock.com; p. 127 Nata Naumovec/Shutterstock.com; p. 128 Journalist/Shutterstock.com; p. 129 joyfull/Shutterstock.com; p. 130 Ahanov Michael/Shutterstock.com; p. 131 DUSAN ZIDAR/Shutterstock.com.

Some of the images in this book illustrate individuals who are models. The depictions do not imply actual situations or events.

CPSIA compliance information: Batch #CS20CSQ: For further information contact Cavendish Square Publishing LLC, New York, New York, at 1-877-980-4450.

Printed in the United States of America

Find us on

CONTENTS

SLOVENIA TODAY

WHAT KIND OF COUNTRY HAS A NATIONAL HOLIDAY IN HONOR of a poet? Schoolchildren have the day off, and many workers do too. This poet is also considered a national hero. What kind of country has a poet for a national hero? For that matter, what kind of country has a comedian running the government as the prime minister? Also, what kind of country chooses as one of its national symbols a blind, cave-dwelling creepy-crawly called a "human fish"? It's Slovenia!

With its alpine mountains, lush forests, mysterious caves, high castles, and bluer-than-the-sky lakes, Slovenia has enough natural beauty to make anyone a poet. Wedged between Italy and Croatia on the Adriatic Sea, it also has a few miles of coastal beaches on its western edge. In the east, the rolling hills and flat grasslands of the Pannonian Plain add yet another kind of geographical scenery to the mix. This is all in a country that's smaller than the state of New Jersey.

Slovenia is a country in the southern part of Central Europe. As an independent nation, it has only existed since 1991. Prior to that, it was part of the much larger federation of states called Yugoslavia, a socialist/communist country that fell

This map shows Slovenia and its neighbors. Note its tiny coastline on the Adriatic Sea between Italy and Croatia.

apart around the same time as the Soviet Union. With the collapse of these huge national entities, smaller countries emerged, seeking independence and identity. Slovenia was one of them. That's one reason why not many people outside of the region may have heard of it—or if they have, they might not know quite where it is.

Complicating matters is the presence of another nation, Slovakia. In a similar scenario, and at around the same time, Slovakia emerged from the dissolution of Czechoslovakia, another socialist federation in Central Europe. Slovenia and Slovakia are often confused for each other, much to the chagrin of the Slovenes (and probably the Slovaks as well). There's also Slavonia, which is not a country unto itself but a large region in eastern Croatia.

If Slovenia has a slight identity problem, it's easy enough to understand why. However, word of its incredible beauty is getting out, and tourists are taking note. Another boost to Slovenia's national publicity came, unexpectedly, following the 2016 US presidential election. The new First Lady of the United States, Melania Trump, was a native-born Slovene. She is only the second First Lady to have been born outside the United States.

Slovenia is rightfully proud of the progress it has made in such a short time since independence. It has transitioned from a communist country to a democratic society and is a prosperous nation with a growing economy. It has enhanced its relationships with its neighbors and forged positive connections with other European countries, particularly France and Germany. It has cultivated close cooperation with the United States and Canada in economic, scientific, and technical matters. It has attained membership in the European Union (EU) and NATO. Slovenia's democratic connections with the West are solid, but it also shares common cultural, historic, and ethnic ties with Russia, Turkey, and the Balkan states and aims for good relations with those nations as well.

Slovenia is a land of peace. In the 2019 Global Peace Index, Slovenia was ranked 8th out of 163 nations. (Iceland was number 1, and Afghanistan was last. The United States came in at number 128.) The Global Peace Index is published by the Institute for Economics and Peace.

With beauty, prosperity, freedom, and peace, Slovenia must be one of the happiest places on Earth. Curiously, though, it isn't. The 2019 World Happiness Report, an annual publication of the UN Sustainable Development Solutions Network, listed Slovenia as the 44th happiest country on Earth. Slovenia was 44th out of 156 countries that were ranked according to various categories meant to reflect happiness levels. The happiest country in the world that year, for the second year in a row, was Finland. While 44th is not a totally miserable finding, Slovenia's placement right between Colombia and Nicaragua seems lower than one might expect. (Although 44th was a 7-point improvement over Slovenia's previous showing!)

A Slovene woman enjoys a happy afternoon with her children in a park.

What accounts for this relatively low ranking? Slovenes scored lowest in the "positive affect" category. It measures the frequency of the respondent's positive feelings of happiness, laughter, and enjoyment on the day prior to the survey. In this, Slovenia ranked 114th. Stereotypes of Slovenes often suggest that Slovenes are dour and humorless. Such a trait cannot possibly be true for all Slovenes, and yet the stereotype persists.

A major concern in Slovenia—one that could possibly be affecting the general happiness of Slovenes—is undocumented migrants. In the 2010s, Europe experienced an unprecedented flood of migrants from war-torn regions in the Middle East and North Africa. In March 2016, Slovenia announced that it would refuse transit to most migrants seeking to travel through the Balkan route to northern Europe. In that part of the world, most migrants were coming from Pakistan, Algeria, Afghanistan, Morocco, and Bangladesh. Syrian refugees fleeing the brutal civil war in their country were also a large contingent. Only a fraction sought asylum in Slovenia; most were just passing through to neighboring Italy or Austria.

In 2018, for example, 2,740 refugees requested asylum in Slovenia, according to the United Nations High Commissioner for Refugees (UNHCR). Most of

In September 2015, police along the border between Slovenia and Croatia watch Syrian refugees while awaiting authorization to open the border.

them came from Pakistan, Algeria, or Afghanistan. Out of 464 decisions that were made on the initial applications, about 19 percent were granted and 81 percent were rejected. Most successful were refugees from Eritrea and from Syria. Meanwhile, the Slovene government has built a fence along parts of its border with Croatia to keep the desperate people out. Most Slovenes agreed with the measure.

The Slovene happiness paradox is noticeable in other data as well. The people of this lovely country suffer a very high suicide rate. In 2019, it was the 11th highest in the world, according to the World Health Organization (WHO). The figures are declining, which is good news, but they are still above the average European Union rate.

Slovenia also has a high rate of alcoholism, particularly in the rural eastern part of the country. In 2018, statistics revealed that alcohol was directly associated with two deaths a day in Slovenia. Road accidents caused by drunk drivers claim an average of 75 lives every year. To some extent, the problem is blamed on the social culture, in which drinking is a way of life. Nevertheless, the government, in concert with the National Institute of Public Heath, has been taking steps to try to rein in the problem. In 2018, the Slovene National Assembly passed a resolution on a 10-year National Mental Health Program aimed at improving access to mental health services for its people. Among other priorities, the resolution includes the creation of more alcohol abuse and suicide prevention programs.

With that sort of positive action being taken to improve life in their country, Slovenes should have much to feel happy about. Perhaps the figures in a few short years will reflect this optimism.

GEOGRAPHY

The Soca River runs through a mountainous region of western Slovenia.

THE NATURAL BEAUTY OF SLOVENIA is seen in its snow-capped mountains, melodic waterfalls, sprawling forests, tranquil lakes, rolling hills, grassy plains, rambling rivers, spectacular caves, and small areas of seashore with sparkling beaches. These diverse landscapes attract tourists but also protect around 50,000 species of animals and 3,000 species of plants.

LOCATION

In Central Europe, Slovenia nestles like a small, jagged piece of a jigsaw puzzle between Austria (to the north), Croatia (to the south), Italy (to the west), and Hungary (to the east). It covers an area of 7,827 square miles (20,273 square kilometers), slightly smaller than the state of New Jersey. A shoreline of 29 miles (46.6 kilometers) is on the Adriatic Sea.

The Julian Alps of northwestern Slovenia rise to heights of over 9,000 feet (2,743 meters). Mount Triglav, the tallest peak in Slovenia, is 9,397 feet (2,864 m) high and offers a spectacular view of deep valleys and wide plateaus. These plateaus extend throughout southwestern and southern Slovenia, a limestone region of underground rivers, gorges, and

1

Slovenia is a heavily forested land. In terms of relative forest cover, Slovenia ranks third in the European Union, after Finland and Sweden, with around 58.2 percent of the country covered by forests and woodlands.

AUSTRIA

HUNGARY

Murska
Sobota

Pesnica

Dravograd

Drava

Lendava

Maribor

Ljutomer

Mura

Slovenj
Gradec

Ptuj

Ormoz

Jesenice

Velenje

Slovenska
Bistrica

Bled

Radovljica

Savinja

Bovec

Celje

Rogaska
Slatina

Kranj

Kamnik

Soca

Tolmin

Trbovlje

ITALY

Domzale

Sava

LJUBLJANA

SLOVENIA

Brezice

Nova
Gorica

Logatec

Krka

■ ZAGREB

Postojna

Novo
Mesto

Sezana

Ribnica

CROATIA

Pivka

Kocevje

Metlika

Piran

Koper

Crnomelj

Izola

Adriatic Sea

Gulf of
Trieste

Kolpa

0   10   20   30 km
0   10   20   30 mi

Slovenia's capital, Ljubljana, other important cities, and major rivers are shown on this map.

caves. Inland from the southern coast of the country are farmlands, which provide a variety of vegetables and fruits. The eastern part of Slovenia is an area of hills separated by large plains of gravel and clay. Central Slovenia is heavily forested. Woodlands cover more than half of Slovenia. Farmlands—fields, orchards, vineyards, and pastures—are sometimes at risk of being overrun by the forests.

There are many rivers in Slovenia. The 181-mile (292 km) Kolpa River runs along much of the border with Croatia. The interior of the country is irrigated by the Sava and the Drava Rivers, which flow eastward into Croatia and ultimately empty into the Danube, one of the major rivers of Europe. The Soca River flows south and briefly crosses into Italy before emptying into the Gulf of Trieste, an offshoot of the Adriatic Sea. Slovenia also has many lakes.

SEASONS AND CLIMATE

Climates in Slovenia vary in the different regions. The Julian Alps and the valleys in the northwest are very cold in winter and pleasantly mild in summer. Farther west, and along the Adriatic coast, autumn and spring offer many warm, sunny days, and the winters are mild. Eastern Slovenia has very hot summers and very cold winters. In the country as a whole, January is the coldest month, with an average daytime temperature of 28 degrees Fahrenheit (—2 degrees Celsius). In July, the average temperature is 70°F (21°C). The average annual precipitation is 31.5 inches (80 centimeters) in the east and as much as 118 inches (300 cm) in the northwest.

Lake Bled in the Julian Alps is a particularly scenic area.

REGIONS

Slovenia is divided geologically into four main regions—the Alpine, the Dinaric, the Mediterranean, and the Pannonian landscapes.

ALPINE   The European Alps cover about two-fifths of the country and are Slovenia's highest elevations. They extend across the north and northwest along the borders with Italy and Austria. The historical name for the central Alpine region is Gorenjska.

DINARIC   The Dinaric Alps make up another mountainous region in the southwest of the country. This range extends from Italy through Slovenia and south to Albania on the Balkan Peninsula. The Dinaric, or Kras, region features a rugged karst terrain, which is characterized by barren, rocky ground, caves, and underground rivers.

MEDITERRANEAN   Western Slovenia is called Primorska. It borders or includes (depending on the map) Slovene Istria, the southern coastal region.

Since 1975, the United Nations Educational, Scientific and Cultural Organization (UNESCO) has maintained a list of international landmarks or regions considered to be of "outstanding value" to the people of the world. Such sites embody the common natural and cultural heritage of humanity, and therefore deserve particular protection. The organization works with the host country to establish plans for managing and conserving their sites. UNESCO also reports on sites that are in imminent or potential danger of destruction and can offer emergency funds to try to save the property.

The organization is continually assessing new sites for inclusion on the World Heritage list. In order to be selected, a site must be of "outstanding universal value" and meet at least one of ten criteria. These required elements include cultural value—that is, artistic, religious, or historical significance—and natural value, including exceptional beauty, unusual natural phenomena, or scientific importance.

As of January 2020, there were 1,121 sites listed, including 869 cultural, 213 natural, and 39 mixed (cultural and natural) properties in 167 nations. Of those, 53 were listed as "in danger."

Slovenia is the location of four UNESCO World Heritage sites—two cultural and two natural sites. The cultural sites are "Heritage of Mercury: Almadén and Idrija," a historic property the country shares with a location in Spain, and "Prehistoric Pile Dwellings Around the Alps," an archaeological designation shared with several other Alpine countries. The natural sites are part of the "Ancient

The beautiful Skocjan Caves are a World Heritage site and a tourist attraction.

and Primeval Beech Forests of the Carpathians and Other Regions of Europe," a trans-boundary property shared with 11 other nations; and the "Skocjan Caves," Slovenia's only exclusive World Heritage site.

It stretches south from the Julian Alps in the north toward the Istrian Peninsula. The coastal region is sometimes called the Slovene Riviera, located on the Gulf of Trieste on the Adriatic Sea. It has a Mediterranean climate on the coast, characterized by hot, humid summers and mild to cold winters.

PANNONIAN Slovenia's northeastern section reaches into Central Europe's great Pannonian Basin. This region, often called the Pannonian Plain, is characterized by flat, grassy lowlands. In Slovenia, this region is called Pomurje (PO-mur-ee-uh), named for the Mura (or Mur) River which flows through it. Its large agricultural plain is known as the Slovene breadbasket. Across the Mura River lies the easternmost part of Slovenia, called Prekmurje (PREK-mur-ee-uh), meaning "over the Mura."

The wide open expanses of the Pannonian Plain define the landscape surrounding the small town of Podova in northeastern Slovenia.

CITIES

Of the approximately 6,000 settlements in Slovenia, 67 are large enough to be considered towns—meaning a settlement with more than 3,000 people. Of those, 16 are cities with more than 10,000 people, with the capital, Ljubljana (loob-lee-AH-na) being by far the largest.

LJUBLJANA The most populous city in Slovenia is the capital, Ljubljana, with a population of about 286,000 in 2018. Ljubljana is a combination of a bustling urban area, a university town with thousands of students, and a throwback to the old Europe of baroque churches, fountains, and sculptures. Its 1,000-year-old castle features a pentagon-shaped tower that offers a breathtaking view of the city, including the gargoyle-fringed rooftops of the district known as Old Town. Looking out beyond the city, the view includes the Julian Alps and the three peaks of Mount Triglav; the mysterious *barje* (marshlands); the brightly lit cafés lining the banks of the Ljubljanica River; and Tivoli Park, with its

The tall buildings of central Ljubljana can be seen in the distance in this view from the city's outskirts.

recreation center featuring bowling alleys, tennis courts, swimming pools, and a roller-skating rink

Ljubljana began as an outpost of the Roman legions in the first century BCE, and there are still ruins testifying to the Roman occupation. In the 14th century, the Hapsburg dynasty of Austria-Hungary took over the city. They built many of the lovely white mansions and churches that are still standing. Napoleon captured the city in 1809 and held it under French rule for five years. During that time, by his order, Ljubljana was the capital of what he called the Illyrian Provinces. Following World War I (1914—1918), the city became part of the newly formed nation of Yugoslavia. It became the capital of Slovenia following the breakaway from Yugoslavia in 1991.

SLOVENJ GRADEC   Nestled between Mount Urslja Gora and the western Pohorje mountain range where the Mislinja and Suhodolnica Rivers meet,

Slovenj Gradec (slo-VEEN grahd-etz) dates back to 1191. A walled city with a rich crafts tradition, its attractions include a gallery of fine arts, the Koroska Regional Museum, and the Soklic Museum. It has four picturesque churches and has maintained, in its original condition, the house where the composer Hugo Wolf was born in 1860. Vodriz Castle stands just outside the city.

Wearing the honorable title of "Peace Messenger City" of the United Nations (UN), Slovenj Gradec holds a yearly Festival of Peace, actively involving the municipal government, the city's schoolchildren, and the United Nations Educational, Scientific and Cultural Organization (UNESCO). Schoolchildren work on UNESCO peace projects throughout the year. Adult citizens' devotion to the cause of nonviolence and peaceful conflict resolution has made Slovenj Gradec a model for peace activists around the world.

KOPER   Behind the district of shipping warehouses that line the harbor, Koper is a city of narrow cobbled streets and winding back alleys. The town square is surrounded on all four sides by interesting buildings. These include the City Tower, the Cathedral of the Assumption, the 12th-century Carmine Rotunda, the 15th-century Praetorian Palace, and the Koper Town Hall. South of the

This aerial photo shows the important port city of Koper.

Slovenia is a country of great natural beauty, and it has taken steps to protect its natural assets. It has created a system of nature parks that cover some 13 percent of its territory.

These include one national park, Triglav National Park; 3 regional parks; 34 landscape parks; and 66 nature reservations. In addition, there are 1,200 natural monuments, 2 geoparks, and numerous botanical gardens.

Rugged, snow-topped mountains are part of Triglav National Park, Slovenia's largest protected area.

Triglav National Park, established in 1981 and named for Slovenia's tallest mountain, Mount Triglav, covers 207,524 acres (83,982 hectares). That is almost all of the Slovene part of the Julian Alps range.

The regional parks include the Skocjan Caves Park, a UNESCO World Heritage site. In addition, there is the Kozjansko Regional Park, an area of landscape diversity bordering the Sotla River in the eastern part of the country, and Notranjska Regional Park, centered on Cerknica Lake, which is an area of diverse plant and bird species and around 450 underground caves.

Other parks include the Ljubljana Marshes Nature Park, a wetlands area where great archaeological treasures have been found. The world's oldest wooden wheel yet discovered, around 5,150 years old, was found there in 2002. The Logar Valley Landscape Park, a glacial valley in the northern Kamnik-Savinja Alps, protects a mountainous landscape of stunning beauty.

square is Shoemakers Street, an avenue of expensive shops. Farther along is Almerigogna Palace, a Venetian gothic structure decorated with Renaissance frescoes. All this is out of sight of the harbor, where cargoes are loaded, ships pull up anchor, and the bustle of commerce defines Slovenia's major seaport.

PTUJ Believed to be the oldest city in Slovenia, Ptuj (p-TOO-ee) is the cultural center of the district of Podravje. The municipal government has assigned landmark status to the city's many historical buildings and monuments to protect them from the wrecking crews of developers. The castle, the Dominican monastery, the old city hall, and the patrician houses with their intricately carved doors, wrought-iron window grilles, and stone-cut facades are all preserved. Three times a year, the residents of Ptuj stage colorful festivals, and costumed revelers dance in the city streets. Every Saturday, musicians gather in front of the city hall to serenade newlyweds.

Old Town Ptuj is known for its distinctive red roofs and for the Ptuj Grad, or castle, which sits on a hill above the Drava River.

Pedestians enjoy a warm day in the center of Maribor.

MARIBOR The second-largest city in Slovenia, Maribor, stands at the crossroads of traffic routes leading from Central Europe. During the last 60 years, it has changed from a provincial town of merchants and craftspeople to an economically dynamic city with a major university. Maribor's winter stadium regularly hosts women's races as part of the Alpine Skiing World Cup. In addition to its varied and historic architecture, Maribor features a national theater where operas are performed, a city park, and an aquarium. Some of the vineyards surrounding Maribor are over 400 years old. The city, along with the Portuguese city of Guimarães, was selected the European Capital of Culture (a European Union designation) for 2012.

NOVA GORICA Often called the Slovene Las Vegas, Nova Gorica (no-vah gor-EETZ-ah) is a relatively new city—unusual in Slovenia—built after World War II (1939—1945). Situated on the Italian border, Nova Gorica attracts many tourists to its gambling casinos and entertainment houses. Its economic development is based on attracting industry and promoting small businesses, many of which are associated with the tourist trade. Discos, which are like clubs in the United States, abound, and for thrill seekers there are parachuting and hang-gliding facilities. The medieval castle of Rihemberk is nearby.

The town of Nova Gorica, near the Italian border, is widely known as a gambling and entertainment destination for tourists.

INTERNET LINKS

https://www.naravniparkislovenije.si/en
Photos and information about many of Slovenia's nature parks are presented on this site.

http://www.slovenia.si/slovenia/country/geography
The official Slovenia tourism site includes information and links pertaining to the country's geography.

https://whc.unesco.org/en/statesparties/si
This is the UNESCO World Heritage listing for Slovenia.

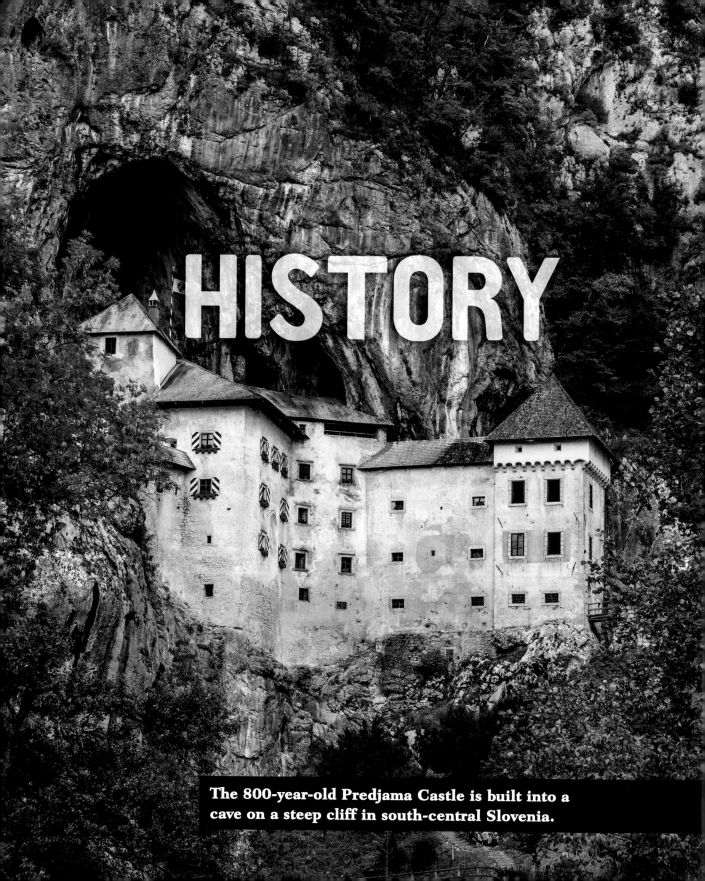

HISTORY

The 800-year-old Predjama Castle is built into a cave on a steep cliff in south-central Slovenia.

2

E ARLY KNOWLEDGE OF THE AREA now known as Slovenia has been lost in the mists of history. There is evidence that the legions of the Roman Empire established settlements there around 10 BCE, but they were later driven out by invading Huns, Goths, and Avars.

In the sixth century CE, the invaders were expelled by Slavs from what would come to be called Eastern Europe. In 623 CE, King Samo established a Slovene kingdom that stretched from Hungary to the Mediterranean Sea. In the year 748, the German-ruled Frankish Empire conquered Slovenia, to be succeeded by the Holy Roman Empire in the ninth century. During this period, the Slovene population was converted to Christianity, becoming part of the Roman Catholic Church. The Austro-German monarchy, which would evolve into the Austro-Hungarian Hapsburg Empire, took over in the 14th century and ruled Slovenia—with one brief interruption—until 1918.

THE HAPSBURGS AND NAPOLEON

Early Austro-German rule was harsh. The Austro-German rulers made the Slovene farmers serfs, who neither owned the estates on which they labored nor profited from them. Upper-class Slovenes conformed to German society and were absorbed into the ruling system, but the majority, who belonged to the lower classes, retained their Slovene identity. Slovenia's Roman Catholic priests were instrumental in the preservation of Slovene culture and worked to encourage pride in Slovenia's heritage.

The ancient kingdom of Noricum, a Celtic civilization, once included Austria and part of Slovenia in the fourth and third centuries BCE. Noricum eventually became a province of the Roman Empire.

In Kobarid, the Napoleon Bridge crosses the Soca River in a region rich with history and scenic beauty.

A series of peasant uprisings took place during the 15th and 16th centuries. These were firmly put down. The condition of the Sloveneian serfs did not improve until the 18th century, when the Austro-Hungarian Hapsburg empress Maria Theresa and her son Joseph II decreed reforms. Further reforms followed in 1809, when the French armies of Napoleon seized Slovenia.

Napoleon's invasion of Slovenia was key to his effort to block the Hapsburg Empire's access to the Adriatic Sea. Napoleon eventually conquered Slovenia, Dalmatia, and part of Croatia, decreeing them France's Illyrian Provinces, with Ljubljana as the capital. He held this area for five years. During that time, the French instituted sweeping reforms in education, law, and the Slovene government. When the Hapsburg administrators returned in 1814, these reforms were firmly in place, and they were unable to dislodge them.

KINGDOM OF SERBS, CROATS, AND SLOVENES

In 1848, democratic revolutions swept across Europe, giving birth to a desire for freedom among Slovenes. Slowly, a movement for political independence from the Hapsburg Empire began to form. However, many years would go by before that dream would be realized. It would take World War I and the breakup of the Austro-Hungarian Empire to release Slovenia from Hapsburg rule.

The First World War Cemetery in Ukanc, Slovenia, is home to the graves of 282 Austro-Hungarian soldiers.

At the end of World War I, in 1918, various areas of what had been the Austro-Hungarian Empire became separate, independent nations. Slovenia became part of the Kingdom of the Serbs, Croats, and Slovenes, ruled by the Serbian Karageorgevic family dynasty. The initial ruler was King Peter I, and when he died after three years on the throne, the crown went to his son, King Alexander I.

The new kingdom was afflicted by high inflation, internal rivalries between Serbs and Croats, and territorial disputes with neighboring countries. In 1929, to avoid chaos, King Alexander imposed a royal dictatorship. That same year, he changed the name of the country from the Kingdom of Serbs, Croats, and Slovenes to the Kingdom of Yugoslavia. Total chaos was avoided, but internal disruptions cropped up constantly during the next five years. These occurred less often, and were generally less violent, in Slovenia than in other parts of Yugoslavia.

WORLD WAR II

In 1934, during a diplomatic visit to Marseilles, France, King Alexander was assassinated by Croatian terrorists. His 11-year-old son, Peter II, became king. Peter's great-uncle, Prince Paul, husband of Princess Olga of Greece,

There are no separate statistics for Slovenia's Jewish population at the start of World War II. Nobody knows how many Slovene Jews died in the Holocaust, but it is estimated that in 1941, before the start of World War II, there were roughly 70,000 Jews throughout Yugoslavia. By the end of 1945, approximately 60,000 had been killed by the Nazis. Many Jews were hunted down, arrested, and sent to concentration camps. Roughly 86 percent of Yugoslavia's Jews perished in the Holocaust. Countless Slovene Jews were among them.

Jews had migrated to Slovenia in the 13th century. As early as 1277, the walled city of Maribor had a "Jewish street" and a synagogue. There were also Jewish communities in the cities of Ptuj, Celje, Radgona, and Ljubljana. However, in 1496, the emperor Maximilian I of Austria drove all Jews out of Slovenia. In the 19th and early 20th centuries, they began drifting back, but it wasn't until the establishment of the Kingdom of Serbs, Croats, and Slovenes that Jews from other parts of the country, where anti-Semitism ran high, migrated in large numbers to Slovenia.

In January 2000, President Milan Kucan of the Republic of Slovenia addressed an international forum on the Holocaust

The narrow "Jewish Street" in the old section of Ljubljana is a reminder of the communities that once lived there.

in Stockholm, Sweden. President Kucan ended his speech by offering the hope that "the Holocaust and the genocide against all nations who fell victim to it, as well as its causes and consequences, [would] find their proper place in the schoolbooks of all democratic countries of the world."

became the prince regent who actually governed Yugoslavia along with two other regents.

World War II broke out in most of Europe in 1939. By 1941, all but one of Yugoslavia's neighbors had fallen to the Nazis. In March 1941, Prince Paul signed a pact with Germany and its ally Italy. Soon after, on March 27, 1941, Prince Paul was removed in a bloodless palace coup. King Peter II, then 18 years old, was able to legally ascend to the throne.

His reign did not last long. Within a week, Germany, Italy, Hungary, and Bulgaria invaded Yugoslavia. The government was forced to surrender, and King Peter had to flee the country. He made his way to London, England, where he set up a Yugoslav government in exile.

Meanwhile, a large part of Slovenia was annexed by Germany, with Italy and Hungary laying claim to the remaining areas. From 1941 through the end of the war in 1945, Slovene partisan groups fought the occupation from bases in the mountains and from underground caves in their country. Toward the end of that same period, with the help of Soviet tank brigades, Serbian partisans drove the Germans from Belgrade, the capital city of Yugoslavia, and established a communist government. The leader of the highly organized and extremely effective communist partisan movement in Yugoslavia was Josip Broz, better known as Tito.

UNDER COMMUNIST RULE

On November 29, 1945, the Federal Republic of Yugoslavia was formed, with Tito at its head. King Peter II had not abdicated, but he had no armies to enforce any effort to reclaim his throne. Tito would rule Yugoslavia for the next 35 years. However, because he refused to follow the Communist Party line dictated by the Soviet Union, Yugoslavia's relations with the United States and other democratic nations were better than those of any other communist country.

During Tito's regime, there was tenfold growth in industrial output between pre–World War II and 1970. Between 1947 and 1980, farm production expanded, and exports of wood products from forests increased. As part of Tito's power grid, many hydroelectric plants were built to harness river power. Increased

Communism is a political, social, and economic philosophy in which all property is publicly owned and each person works and is paid by the government according to their abilities and needs, as determined by the government. This doctrine is the opposite of liberal democracy and capitalism.

Josip Broz, the communist dictator of Yugoslavia, better known as Tito, was born into a peasant family on May 7, 1892, in Kumrovec, Croatia. The 7th of 15 children, he was apprenticed to a locksmith at an early age. In 1910, in Vienna, Austria, Broz joined the Social Democratic Party. Drafted into the Austro-Hungarian army in 1913, he fought in World War I, was captured by the Russians, and spent time in a prisoner-of-war camp.

After the war, Broz married Pelagija Beloussowa, and in 1920, he joined the Communist Party of Yugoslavia (KPJ). He worked as a union agitator and was sentenced to five years in the penitentiary for his communist activity. Released in 1934, he went underground and adopted the alias of Tito.

President Tito waves to the crowd during the May Day Parade in 1955.

In 1941, when the Nazis and their allies occupied Yugoslavia, Tito organized the communist partisan resistance movement. In 1943, Tito was wounded in combat and named marshal of Yugoslavia. In 1945, as the war drew to a close, Tito organized a new Yugoslav government and was appointed prime minister.

In November 1945, without putting it to a vote by the people, Tito illegally abolished the monarchy. Yugoslavia, including Slovenia, was now a one-party state—the Federal Republic of Yugoslavia—under the communist leadership of Prime Minister Tito.

In 1948, Soviet leader Joseph Stalin expelled Tito and Yugoslavia from the world communist movement after Tito started showing signs of independence. In 1953, Tito was named president as well as prime minister. In 1974, he was named "president for life." After 35 years as the dictator of Yugoslavia, Tito died at the age of 88 in Ljubljana, on May 4, 1980.

Domestically, Tito's greatest accomplishment was keeping the lid on the animosity between the Serbs of Bosnia-Herzegovina and the Croats of Croatia, whose violent feuding preceding World War I was heightened by pro- and anti-Nazi actions during World War II. This tension would break into full-scale war during the years following Tito's death.

tourism contributed to the economy. Under Tito, the entire population of Yugoslavia was covered by health insurance.

The bubble burst in 1979. A worldwide oil crisis caused a lasting shock to the Yugoslav industrial development strategy when the price of fuel to run the country's factories skyrocketed. Between 1975 and 1980, inflation reached an annual rate of 50 percent. By the time Tito died in 1980, his communist policies were already becoming unpopular with the Yugoslav people.

THE INDEPENDENCE MOVEMENT

Following Tito's death, the communist system in Yugoslavia began to crumble. In 1982, the Kraigher Commission, assigned to come up with recommendations for dealing with the collapsing economy, released plans for a long-term economic stabilization program. Among their recommendations was a wage austerity program that reduced workers' salaries. The Yugoslav Federal Assembly passed only 8 of the 25 Kraigher Commission proposals.

Attempts by the communist government to shift capital from rich areas to poor areas aroused particular resentment in Slovenia. Feelings ran high that Slovenes should not have to pay forever for Yugoslav regions such as Macedonia, Kosovo, Montenegro, and Bosnia, where the people had not developed profitable industries.

In 1987, a small but influential group of intellectuals called for Slovenia to replace the communist system with a democratic system, to establish a free-market economy while maintaining public welfare policies, and to declare independence from Yugoslavia. The proposal caught on with the Slovene people, and in May 1989, there was a large rally in Ljubljana to support it.

By November, political parties—the Democratic Alliance of Slovenia, the Social Democrat Alliance of Slovenia, the Slovene Christian Democrats, the Farmer's Alliance, the Greens of Slovenia, and others—had formed and united into the Democratic Opposition of Slovenia (DEMOS). DEMOS won control of the Slovene parliament in the April 1990 election. Later that year, a national vote on independence for Slovenia was held. An unusually large turnout resulted in 88.2 percent in favor of independence. On June 25, 1991, the Slovene parliament enacted the Declaration of Independence of the Republic of Slovenia, severing the nation from Yugoslavia. Milan Kucan became the country's first president.

THE 10-DAY WAR

The Yugoslav government opposed allowing Slovenia to secede. The Yugoslav army (YNA) occupied Slovenia's border crossings, cutting the country off from the outside world while maintaining Yugoslav sovereignty over it. Plans were underway to replace the rebellious government of Slovenia. Slovenia responded.

The government organized local territorial defense forces. Police units from various cities were organized. YNA units were blocked from areas they tried to occupy. They were attacked by local militia and police. Large numbers of Slovene citizens not only resisted the YNA but also fought pitched battles with them. After two days, with the Slovene resistance taking its toll, the YNA threatened retaliatory measures against the civilian population. Throughout

A convoy of Yugoslav army tanks moves through a rural region during the war in Slovenia. The distance to Zagreb is listed on the road sign.

most of Europe, public opinion sided with Slovenia. The European Community sent three diplomats to Zagreb, Yugoslavia, to try to arrange a cease-fire. As the conflict heated up, a delegation headed by Ante Markovic, the Yugoslav federal prime minister, arrived in Zagreb. By then, the YNA had effectively been defeated in Slovenia. Yugoslavia had no choice but to agree to a cease-fire. The armistice decreed that Slovenia would retain control over its territory, including its borders; that trapped YNA units would be allowed to move out; that all prisoners of war on both sides would be released; and that for three months Slovenia would refrain from any further measures designed to finalize its independence. The 10-Day War was over.

SLOVENE NATIONHOOD

By October 8, 1991, the three-month cooling-off period had passed, the Yugoslav nation was breaking up, and Slovenia began efforts to secure recognition from other nations as an independent state. In January of the following year, the European Community recognized Slovenia. Recognition by the United States followed in April. In May, Slovenia was accepted into the United Nations and admitted to the Council of Europe.

Following independence, the DEMOS ruling coalition began to unravel. There were heated debates between socialist-leaning liberals and strict Catholic conservatives regarding the wording of the new constitution and the privatization of property that had been held publicly under the communist regime. Nevertheless, an agreement was reached, and by the end of 1991, a democratic constitution had been adopted.

In December 1992, elections were held. DEMOS was defeated, with the Liberal Democrat Party (LDS) winning enough votes (23 percent) to form a centrist coalition government. This included the Christian Democrats and two center-left socialist democratic parties. The bills passed by the coalition halted the downward slide in wages, established rules for privatization, rehabilitated banks, and established rules for elections. These stabilized the country and established its soundness among other nations.

Throughout the 1990s, as the other former territories of Yugoslavia were engaged in fierce civil war among Serbs, Croats, and Bosnians, Slovenia remained peaceful. The Slovenes focused on building a free-market economy, improving the nation's infrastructure, attracting foreign investment, perfecting a national health system, reducing unemployment, successfully reducing inflation, and improving agricultural production. These efforts were ongoing as the 21st century began, and in December 2002, an International Monetary Fund (IMF) report concluded that the Slovene economy showed "considerable resilience."

THE 21ST CENTURY

In a 2003 referendum, the Slovene people voiced their approval for membership in both the European Union and NATO. By 2004, Slovenia joined both organizations—a hearty rejection of communism and Russian influence—thereby becoming a full-fledged member of the European Community. In 2007, Slovenia became the first former communist state to adopt the single European currency, the euro.

The global recession of 2008 to 2009 hit Slovenia hard, and the country's economy struggled with growing unemployment through 2013. In 2012, Prime Minister Janez Jansa of the center-right Slovene Democratic Party (SDS) introduced a series of austerity measures intended to reduce the budget

Demonstrators sing as they hold placards and candles during an antigovernment protest in Ljubljana on December 21, 2012.

deficit. These included wage cuts for public sector workers and the abolition or reduction of certain worker benefits, including sick leave, maternity pay, and childcare benefits. The people balked. Tens of thousands of protesters took to the streets of Ljubljana and Maribor to demonstrate against the proposals. A political crisis ensued, complicated by a series of corruption scandals.

In 2013, the Slovene parliament ousted Jansa and installed Alenka Bratusek of the Positive Slovenia Party as prime minister. She was the first woman to hold that office; however, she only lasted about one year. In 2014, she resigned her position after losing the leadership of her party. Miro Cerar became prime minister, heading a center-left coalition, but he, too, resigned his post in 2018.

By 2014, the economy was improving, and unemployment fell significantly by 2018. Politically, the government upheaval of the previous few years produced its first minority government, a center-left coalition led by Prime Minister Marjan Sarec. Meanwhile, the formerly disgraced prime minister Janez Jansa gained renewed political prominence in 2018 despite being given a three-month suspended jail sentence for insulting two female journalists.

INTERNET LINKS

https://www.bbc.com/news/world-europe-17847681
BBC News presents a timeline of key events in the history of Slovenia beginning in 1918.

https://slovenia.si/this-is-slovenia/important-dates-for-slovenia
The Slovene information site presents milestones in the country's history, beginning in 250,000 BCE.

GOVERNMENT

Prime Minister Marjan Sarec arrives for a
European Union summit meeting at the EU
headquarters in Brussels in May 2019.

3

S INCE BREAKING AWAY FROM Yugoslavia in 1991, Slovenia has had a remarkably stable government. There have been a few political ups and downs to be sure, but nothing that has seriously threatened the nation. Since declaring its independence, Slovenia has built a stable democratic political system—holding free elections, instituting a free press, and maintaining a positive record on human rights issues. It's the most prosperous republic of the former Yugoslavia and maintains close ties with the West.

Slovenia is a democratic republic with a parliamentary system. The nation's authority is shared by executive, legislative, and judicial branches. As is usual in a parliamentary system, the nation is led by both a president and a prime minister. As opposed to having a single executive, as is the case in a presidential system (such as in the United States), a parliamentary system divides the role into two. The president is the head of state, and the prime minister is the head of government. The two positions are not equal in power; the prime minister holds the most power, while the president's role is largely ceremonial.

Marjan Sarec, who became Slovenia's prime minister in 2018, began his career as a comedian. He worked as an actor and political satirist on radio and television. His stage persona was a grouchy rural guy. Sarec also did impressions of well-known local and international people. Despite his comedy, the prime minister has assured the nation that he takes political leadership very seriously.

THE CONSTITUTION

As the fundamental law of the Republic of Slovenia, the constitution spells out the rights and responsibilities of citizens, the structure of the government, and the procedures for amending, or changing, the constitution. The document was adopted on December 23, 1991, and remains in effect. It has been amended several times, most recently in 2015.

That most recent amendment, as an example, concerns the right to drinking water. Article 70a reads, "Everyone has the right to drinking water. Water resources shall be a public good managed by the state. As a priority and in a sustainable manner, water resources shall be used to supply the population with drinking water and water for household use and in this respect shall not be a market commodity. The supply of the population with drinking water and water for household use shall be ensured by the state directly through self-governing local communities and on a not-for-profit basis."

Among other things, the constitution assures that "the state shall protect human rights and fundamental freedoms" within its own territory. It further specifies that "[the state] shall protect and guarantee the rights of the autochthonous Italian and Hungarian national communities." ("Autochthonous" means the community has always lived in the country rather than being descended from migrants.) These rights are spelled out in Article 64 and include the right to education in their own languages.

The document guarantees equal rights before the law, regardless of "national origin, race, sex, language, religion, political or other conviction, material standing, birth, education, social status, disability, or any other personal circumstance." Under Article 51, Slovene citizens have a right to health care. Science and the arts are protected in Article 59. In Article 72, everyone is granted the right to a healthy living environment. Free enterprise is also protected, as is the workers' right to strike.

The constitution guarantees freedom of speech, assembly, and religion, among other freedoms. It establishes a separation of church and state. It ensures a right to vote, with universal suffrage beginning at age 18. The constitution bans capital punishment (the death sentence) and torture.

THE EXECUTIVE

The president is the head of state and is elected for a five-year term by direct vote of the Slovene people. He or she may be reelected for a second consecutive five-year term, but not a third consecutive term. After a term out of office, however, he or she is eligible to serve again. The president represents Slovenia in its dealing with other world leaders and is commander in chief of the nation's military forces.

Borut Pahor, the president of Slovenia, holds a press conference in Brussels after meeting with European Union officials in February 2019.

The prime minister is the head of government and is nominated by the party that receives the most votes in a parliamentary election and then appointed to office by the president. He or she has authority over the Council of Ministers (the cabinet) and the government administrative units. The prime minister reports on government decisions and actions to the National Assembly, and is responsible to it.

THE LEGISLATURE

Slovenia has a bicameral, or two-house, legislature (also known as a parliament) made up of the National Assembly and the National Council.

NATIONAL ASSEMBLY (DRZAVNI ZBOR)   The National Assembly has 90 members who serve four-year terms. Of these, 88 are directly elected by the people in single-seat constituencies, and 2 are directly elected in special constituencies for Italian and Hungarian minorities (1 each) by simple majority vote; those members also serve four-year terms. The National Assembly's role is to draft and adopt laws.

THE NATIONAL COUNCIL (DRZAVNI SVET)   The National Council is made up of 40 members indirectly elected by an electoral college every five years. Twenty-two members represent local interests, and 18 members represent

THE FATHER OF HIS COUNTRY

Milan Kucan, the first president of the independent Republic of Slovenia, was born on January 14, 1941, in the village of Prekmurje. Three months later, on April 17, 1941, the Nazis invaded Yugoslavia and occupied Slovenia. Milan's father, a schoolteacher, became an officer in the Slovene resistance movement against the Nazis and was killed fighting them.

Although Slovenia was overwhelmingly Catholic, Kucan was raised a Protestant. He attended primary and secondary school in Murska Sobota, then went to the University of Ljubljana, graduating in 1964 with a degree in law. He became a member of the Central Council of the League of Communists of the Republic of Slovenia in 1969 and served through 1973. During this time, he helped to prepare the constitutional amendments that brought about more decentralization in Tito's Yugoslavia.

In 1978, Kucan became president of the Slovene Assembly. Following Tito's death in 1980, he worked to improve ethnic relations among the diverse groups in Yugoslavia and to have the Communist Party cede more political power to the people. In 1986, Kucan became president of the League of Communists of Slovenia (ZKS) and pushed through measures to reform the organization. Under his leadership, the ZKS initiated a multiparty system that brought democracy to Slovenia. Although he was still a Communist, in 1986 he insisted that the people must have a genuine political voice in government, a voice not limited by party domination.

While it was still part of Yugoslavia, Slovenia held its first multiparty elections in 1990, and Kucan became president. He presided over the declaration of Slovene independence from Yugoslavia and over the 10-Day War that ensued. Following the establishment of the independent Republic of Slovenia, the former Communist Kucan, running as an independent candidate with no party affiliation, was elected the new country's first president in 1992. He was reelected as an independent in 1997, winning 55.54 percent of the votes against seven opponents.

As president, Kucan achieved a wide consensus among Slovenia's rival political parties. He is credited with rebuilding his country economically and with leading it back into democracy. Since leaving office, he has remained involved in international affairs. Among other activities, Kucan has served as a member of the European Council on Tolerance and Reconciliation, a not-for-profit organization established in 2008 to monitor tolerance in Europe. The group advises governments on fighting xenophobia and intolerance on the continent.

special interests—4 members represent employers; 4 represent employees; 4 represent farming, crafts and trades, and independent professions; and 6 represent noncommercial fields. The National Council's role is strictly advisory. It can propose laws to the National Assembly or ask that body to reconsider laws it has passed, but it cannot itself enact legislation.

THE JUDICIAL SYSTEM

There are 201 administrative divisions, called municipalities, in Slovenia. Of these, 11 are considered urban municipalities, or cities, while the others are towns, villages, or rural areas. All have local self-government with elected officials. All are subject to judicial authority by district and regional courts. Their judgments may be upheld or overruled by appeals courts or by the Supreme Court of the Republic of Slovenia.

Criminal cases are brought by the local office of the state prosecutor of Slovenia. An ombudsman for human rights and fundamental freedoms, elected by the National Assembly for a period of six years, may intervene in cases in which rights under the Slovene constitution are called into question. Such cases go before judges of the Constitutional Court, who have the expertise to decide on constitutional issues.

INTERNET LINKS

https://www.gov.si/en/state-authorities/government
Up-to-date information can be found on the Republic of Slovenia government site.

https://slovenia.si/this-is-slovenia/illustrated-constitution-for-young-people/
Lively graphic elements explain the Slovene constitution.

https://www.us-rs.si/media/constitution.pdf
This is a PDF of the constitution of Slovenia in English, provided by the Republic of Slovenia Constitutional Court.

ECONOMY

In the port city of Koper, containers of export goods are loaded onto ships.

4

SINCE BECOMING INDEPENDENT, Slovenia has successfully made the conversion from communism to capitalism. That in itself is a daunting task, being a political as well as economic transition. For the most part, the nation has maintained a healthy economy— though, like most other countries, it suffered economically during the global financial crisis of 2008 to 2009. Since climbing out of that recession, however, its economy has grown. Today, it has one of the strongest economies in Central Europe, and certainly the strongest of the former Yugoslav republics.

This is not surprising. Although Slovenia made up only about one-eleventh of Yugoslavia's total population, it was the most productive of the six republics. It accounted for one-fifth of Yugoslavia's gross domestic product (GDP) and one-third of its exports. Slovenia therefore entered into independence with an already fairly prosperous economy. In addition, it had strong market ties to the West, which it actively built upon. It joined the European Union in 2004 and adopted the euro as its currency in 2007.

Since joining the eurozone in 2007, Slovenia no longer uses its old currency, the tolar. The eurozone, or euro area, is the monetary union of European Union member states that have adopted the euro (€) as their common currency. Some EU members continue to use their own national currencies, although most have plans to adopt the euro in the future.

Gross domestic product (GDP) is a measure of a country's total production. The number reflects the total value of goods and services produced over one year. Economists use it to determine whether a country's economy is growing or contracting. Growth is good, while a falling GDP means trouble. Dividing the GDP by the number of people in the country determines the GDP per capita (per person). This number provides an indication of a country's average standard of living—the higher the better.

In 2017, the GDP per capita in Slovenia was approximately $34,500. That figure is considered fairly strong, and it ranked Slovenia 58th out of 228 countries listed by the CIA World Factbook. For comparison, the United States that year was number 19, with a GDP per capita of $59,500. Neighboring Croatia, also a former republic of Yugoslavia, was number 81, with $24,700. Meanwhile, Serbia was number 111, with a GDP per capita of $15,100.

The government established and encouraged private rather than public ownership, increased and stabilized the value of its currency, reined in inflation, halted rising unemployment, and modernized its taxation system. With its excellent infrastructure, a well-educated workforce, and a strategic location between the Balkans and Western Europe, Slovenia has put its economic advantages to good use. Its GDP has grown steadily, climbing about 5 percent in 2017. Of its total economic output, services make up the highest percentage (65.9 percent) of GDP, followed by industry (32.2 percent) and agriculture (1.8 percent).

SERVICES

Those enterprises accounting for the major part of Slovenia's GDP include so many diverse activities that they might as well be classified as nonindustrial, nonagricultural endeavors rather than services. Among them are telecommunication companies; legal, architectural, construction, and engineering firms; social services such as health care; wholesaling, retailing, and franchising enterprises; schools, colleges, and universities; accounting and advertising businesses; railway and trucking firms; utility companies; travel and tourism services; and many others.

TOURISM

Tourism is a major Slovene service industry, and it's growing rapidly. In 2018, the sector contributed 12 percent of the country's GDP. That year, around 4.4 million foreign tourists visited Slovenia, an 11 percent leap over the previous year. Those guests stayed longer as well, generating a 15 percent rise in the number of overnight stays.

Most visitors were from Italy or Germany (12 percent each), or Austria (9 percent), with the Netherlands and Croatia following with 5 percent each. Outside of Europe, the greatest number of tourists came from the United States. The Slovenian Tourism Board (STO) said 2018 was the fifth consecutive record-breaking year for tourism in Slovenia.

A tour guide leads a group of tourists through the old section of Ljubljana.

The slopes of Vogel Ski Resort, on the outskirts of Triglav National Park, provide a magical setting for visitors.

The ski slopes are a main attraction, as are the more than 4,350 miles (7,000 km) of marked mountain trails for hiking and climbing. Some tourists come for the health benefits of the thermal mineral waters of Slovenia's 15 natural spas. Others are attracted by the 15 miles (24 km) of underground passages of the Postojna Caves, with their otherworldly stalagmites and stalactites. Lakes Bled and Bohinj in the shadow of the Alps, the Adriatic seacoast, and the Lipica stud farms, where the royal Lipizzaner horses are bred, are also major attractions. Busing, housing, feeding, and arranging itineraries for foreign and domestic tourists provide work for many Slovenes.

INDUSTRY

Major industries in Slovenia produce electrical equipment, processed foods, textiles, paper products, chemicals, and wood products. Coal is the most abundant natural resource. There are also facilities to mine lead, zinc, mercury, uranium, and silver, as well as modest amounts of natural gas and petroleum.

The automobile industry is important in Slovenia, contributing to about 20 percent of its exports and 10 percent of GDP. The industry includes more than 60 companies and research institutions. Revoz is one of Slovenia's biggest companies and is its only car manufacturer. As a subsidiary of the French auto company Renault, Revoz produces the Renault models Twingo and Clio out of its assembly plant in Novo Mesto.

AGRICULTURE

Farm and ranch families have a hard life in Slovenia. With some exceptions, the climate and terrain are not hospitable to crops and do not make for good grazing lands for livestock. In the southwestern and northeastern regions of the country, where temperatures soar, there is serious drought during the summer months.

Sheep enjoy grazing in a flowery meadow near a farm in the mountains.

Only 8.4 percent of the land of Slovenia is arable. Raising animals for meat is the most productive sector of Slovene agriculture. Field crops are cultivated mainly for forage by cattle, but also for sheep, goats, and pigs. The next most successful use of land is for orchards and vineyards. Fruit grows on 4 percent of all agricultural land and constitutes between 3 percent and 5 percent of agricultural production. Apples are the main fruit crop, followed by pears, peaches, and cherries. Fruit can also be used for wine, and roughly 35 percent of Slovene farms supplement their income by bottling and selling wine. A small percentage of land is hospitable to barley, corn, potato, soybean, wheat, and sugar beet production.

Slightly more than 2 percent of the Slovene population is involved in farming or ranching. There are few agribusinesses, and small family farms are the rule. The average size of a Slovene farm is 8 acres (3.2 ha). Overgrowing of farmland by Slovene forests is a serious problem. According to the Slovene Ministry of Agriculture, Forestry, and Food, there has been an increase in abandoned farms and overgrown farmlands. The low incomes of farmers, and their low social status, have persuaded many of the next generation to reject farm life. This, according to the ministry, could create future problems in meeting the nation's produce needs.

Slovenia cannot produce enough food to feed its people and therefore must import it, which adds to its cost. Farms produce less than 20 percent of the country's fruit consumption, less than 40 percent of its vegetables, and less than 60 percent of its cereals, sugar, and pork.

TRANSPORTATION

There are sixteen airports in Slovenia, of which seven have paved runways. Ljubljana, Maribor, and Portoro are the three international airports. Flights from Ljubljana regularly connect with all major European airports. Adria Airways was the Slovene national carrier, but it ceased operations in September 2019 after declaring bankruptcy. At that time, Slovenia's economic development minister said the government was considering creating a new national airline, Air Slovenia, to be launched as soon as possible. In the meantime, Brussels Airlines, Lufthansa, and Swiss jumped in to add flights to Ljubljana to take up the slack.

Slovene railways cover 764 miles (1,229 km) and crisscross the country to reach all major Slovene cities. Offshoots of the four main lines from Ljubljana in the center of Slovenia split off at various points to cover the nation. At key transfer points, they connect with each other. There are links to all the major railways of Europe.

The country's road network extends over 24,224 miles (38,985 km), providing access to all but the most remote regions of the country. All major roads are paved, including 478 miles (769 km) of expressways.

Entry to Slovenia from the Adriatic Sea is through the ports of Koper, Izola, and Piran.

INTERNET LINKS

https://www.slovenia.info/en/things-to-do/spas-and-health-resorts
Slovenia's spas and health resorts are presented on this tourism site.

https://www.stat.si/Popis2011/eng/default.aspx
The Statistical Office of Slovenia reports economic data.

https://www.stat.si/StatWeb/en/news/Index/7978
Tourism statistics for 2018 are offered on this page of the Statistical Office site.

https://www.total-slovenia-news.com/news/business
Various articles relating to business and economic news can be found on this news site.

ENVIRONMENT

The bridge at Vintgar Gorge offers a peaceful natural experience over the clear waters of the Radovna River.

5

PROTECTING THE ENVIRONMENT IS an important challenge in Slovenia, as it is in every nation. Pollution and climate change are major concerns, as are land management and municipal waste generation and treatment. The good news is that Slovenia is making progress in addressing these issues. The country has several motivating factors influencing its policies and actions.

For one thing, the right to live in a healthy environment is guaranteed in Slovenia's constitution. Article 72 states, "Everyone has the right in accordance with the law to a healthy living environment. The state shall promote a healthy living environment. To this end, the conditions and manner in which economic and other activities are pursued shall be established by law."

Slovenia is also party to numerous international agreements and protocols covering a wide range of environmental concerns. Essentially, Slovenia has agreed to abide by certain standards designed to combat pollution and other practices harmful to land, air, water, and animals. Some of these originate through its membership in the European Union, the United Nations, and other associations.

Health statistics provide another incentive for cleaning up environmental problems. The health effects of air pollution, for example, can be quantified in statistics relating to premature deaths. That is, scientists can determine the number of people in a given population who die before reaching their standard life expectancy because of diseases attributable to breathing polluted air. Aside from being a human tragedy, lost lives also cause considerable economic impacts by increasing medical costs and reducing productivity through lost working days.

AIR POLLUTION

Air pollution is one of Slovenia's greatest environmental concerns, and particulate matter and ozone are the largest problems. Particulate matter is a complex concentration of dust, soot, smoke, and other tiny particles and liquid droplets floating in the air. Ozone is a gas with the chemical formula O_3 that is both a natural and human-made product. Depending on where it is in the atmosphere, ozone affects life on Earth in either good or bad ways. In the upper atmosphere, it occurs naturally in small amounts and protects life on Earth from the sun's ultraviolet radiation. In the lower atmosphere, ozone

Smog hangs over the industrial stacks of the Ljubljana Valley.

is created by chemical reactions between air pollutants from vehicle exhaust, gasoline vapors, and other emissions. At ground level, high concentrations of ozone are toxic to people and plants.

In some areas, the country's terrain aggravates the effects of air pollution. Typical is the northern region of Koroska, where factory production has mushroomed in already populated valleys. Air pollution from smokestacks is held in these valleys by the surrounding mountains like water in a basin. Respiratory ailments prevail, and the forest system of the valleys is being threatened by acid rain. The Zasavje coal mining region known as the Black District, with its lack of adequate smoke suppression equipment, also suffers greatly from industrial air pollution. Even the Adriatic seaport of Koper is beset by air pollution, as well as other pollution problems. The problems originate with the metallurgical and chemical plants in the area.

Traffic in Ljubljana becomes congested on the highway to the coast.

Although Slovenia is a small country, it is situated at the crossroads of some of Europe's major transit routes, and freight transport makes up a good portion of that traffic. Emissions from the road transit traffic are the greatest source of air pollution. Air pollution is also caused by domestic heating, especially in densely populated areas. Outdated furnaces and a heavy reliance on burning wood during the cold winters contribute to the particulate matter in the air.

The good news is that Slovenia's air quality has improved over recent years. Awareness of the problem has grown, extending even to children, with many schools using classroom materials developed for all grade levels to receive and analyze data on air pollution.

SLOVENIA'S VANISHED GLACIERS

The snow-capped peak of Mount Triglav, Slovenia's highest mountain, is not only a scenic landmark, it's also a symbol of the country itself. A stylized picture of the mountaintop appears on the country's coat of arms and on its flag.

The Triglav Glacier had been a permanent fixture on that peak, covering more than 100 acres (45 ha) on its northeastern side. However, that was more than a century ago. Over the course of the 20th century, the glacier shrunk in size, and by 2019, it was no longer considered a glacier at all— another victim of climate change. Slovenia's only other glacier, the Skuta Glacier, is shrinking as well, though it has been less sensitive to changing temperatures due to its shadier location.

A man hikes on the Skuta Glacier during the summertime in the Kamnik-Savinja Alps.

CLIMATE CHANGE

There isn't a country on Earth that isn't being affected by climate change. The average annual temperature increase in Slovenia is greater than the global average. This is already causing a change in seasonal precipitation patterns, with more heat waves and droughts. Endemic species may not be able to adapt to these weather changes. Slovenia's agriculture will suffer if adaptations aren't made, and the nation's winter sports tourism sector will be adversely affected.

FORESTS

Forests cover at least 58.2 percent of the land area of Slovenia, and 70 percent of the woodlands are privately owned. Small farmers who own patches of

woodlands, or whose fields touch public woodlands, have traditionally chopped the trees into logs for construction and firewood. They have made furniture and built houses from the products of neighboring woodlands—whether they owned them or not. They have heated their houses and barns with split logs and sold the leftovers to others. Many of them have cleared forests and used the land for grazing cattle. They have gathered fruits, nuts, berries, herbs, and mushrooms for their tables, and regularly peddled the excess for income.

The Forest Development Program of Slovenia (FDPS) is charged with managing the nation's woodlands on the basis of ecologically sound land-use plans. It acts on the basis of the Helsinki Resolutions signed at the Ministerial Conference on the Protection of Forests in Europe in 1993. The Slovenia Forest Service monitors the forests and prepares growth and clearing plans for specific forest areas; assists the owners in selecting trees to be chopped

Nature lovers enjoy a walk through the forest canopy in Rogla, Slovenia.

Slovenia is part of the European Union's Natura 2000, a network of natural protected areas. It covers 18 percent of the EU's land area and almost 9.5 percent of its marine territory, and it stretches across all the EU countries. Natura 2000 is the largest coordinated system of nature conservation in the world. While its aim is to ensure the long-term survival of Europe's most valuable and threatened species and habitats, its more than 27,000 sites are not the same as national parks, though there is some overlap. In fact, much of the land under Natura 2000 jurisdiction is privately owned. The EU program supports sustainable conservation, largely centered on people working with nature rather than against it. However, local populations are not always enthusiastic about upholding its directives, such as limitations on development.

Upon entry to the EU, each member country selects its own areas for Natura 2000 protection. These areas are chosen because they are home to endangered, vulnerable, rare, or endemic species, or because they are exceptional examples of the typical features of one or more of Europe's nine biogeographical regions. These include various types of ecosystems, including terrestrial, freshwater, and marine ecosystems. Around 2,000 species and 230 habitat types are considered appropriate to be designated for Natura 2000 protection.

Slovenia has dedicated 355 Natura 2000 sites for a total area of 2,967 square

This view shows the autumnal colors of Lake Cerknica in southwestern Slovenia.

miles (7,684 sq km). Altogether, the sites encompass 37.16 percent of the country, which is the highest rate of all EU members.

down; conducts education and training sessions for foresters, forest owners, and forest workers; and consults with environmental groups, hunting clubs, hiking clubs, and concerned rural area representatives. Care is taken to see that specific kinds of trees are protected and that a balance is maintained among the species of trees and other plant growth of an area. The feeding habits and population growth of wildlife are also taken into consideration.

All forest owners, no matter how small their property, are required to manage their woodlands in accordance with the FDPS guidelines. They are entitled to government support in these endeavors.

FARMS

In some larger nations, small farms are becoming a thing of the past, but massive, industrial farming has not caught on in Slovenia. The output of the average Slovene farm of 8 acres (3.2 ha), a quarter the size of the average farm in the European Union, is simply too small to compete on the world

Cows graze outside herdsmen's huts on the Big Pasture Plateau in the Kamnik-Savinja Alps near the town of Kamnik, Slovenia.

market. As a result, Slovenia's agricultural sector has declined in recent years as small farmers leave family farms for other lines of work. Arable land is increasingly being developed, replaced by construction projects, roads, and other transportation infrastructure.

To reverse these trends, the government has tried to revive rural areas through policy initiatives and subsidies to support eco-farming and encouraging eco-tourism. Organic farming is slowly catching on as the market demand increases. In 2018, there were 3,320 organic farms registered in Slovenia, a 4 percent increase over 2017. Nevertheless, organic producers represented a mere 4.8 percent of all farms in Slovenia.

PROTECTING THE CAVES

Sewage and other waste products are an ongoing threat to the famous 25-mile (40 km) stretch of 522 caves in Slovenia. Once pollution enters the waters of the caves, it disappears extremely quickly underground and enters the groundwater, which spreads it throughout the underground labyrinth. This

A natural bridge leading to a cave is one of many scenic wonders in Rakov Skocjan, a wild karst valley formed by the Rak River.

threatens the very existence of the creatures that inhabit the caves. Whole species have been lost due to water pollution.

This pollution leaks into cave waters from waste dumps, bathroom wastewater, industrial oil spills, gasoline leaks from cars, and overfertilized soil on nearby farms. Illegal dumping of waste (including both industrial and domestic waste) into cave shafts is also a cause of the pollution.

Not just the caves are at risk. The amount of waste generated in Slovenia is increasing. Waste products from industrial production are particularly hazardous. While some of these are deposited in small landfills and storage facilities inside the properties of the companies that generate them, this is only a temporary solution. The government has taken action that calls for chemical analysis of waste and decreed that only processed waste material may be disposed of at garbage dumps. It has also set up strict conditions for creating new, heavily lined dumps to ensure that liquids don't leak into the soil and pollute underground water sources. The government is allocating additional funding for waste disposal, but it continues to be a major problem for Slovenia.

INTERNET LINKS

https://ec.europa.eu/environment/nature/natura2000
This is the official site of Natura 2000.

http://kazalci.arso.gov.si/sl
When translated, this Slovene government site provides a great deal of information and statistics about environmental issues.

https://www.rtvslo.si/news-in-english/slovenia-revealed/slovenia-s-vanishing-glaciers/360457
This article discusses the disappearance of Slovenia's glaciers.

SLOVENES

A woman rides a bike down a cobblestone street in the city center of Ljubljana.

SLOVENIA IS A SMALL COUNTRY, with about 2.1 million people. About half of them live in urban areas, and the rest live in the nearly 6,000 small towns and villages that are spread across the country. Slovenia is not very crowded; compared to other European nations, its population density is low.

Precise, up-to-date information on demographics is unavailable, and most population figures are estimates that vary according to source. The 2002 Slovene census reported a population of approximately 1,964,000 people. Of those, about 83 percent were ethnic Slovenes; 2 percent were Serbs; 1.8 percent, Croats; 1.1 percent, Bosnians; and 12 percent were other or unspecified. Slovenia's 2011 census was register-based, rather than conducted door-to-door. This approach was done to save government money during a time of economic hardship. A register-based census is a method of producing data on population by linking together existing data sources. The 2002 results are therefore often cited as the most recent census data available. (At this writing, it is unclear how the Slovene government will conduct the next census, due in 2021.)

6

TREE TRUNK TRIBUTE OR PROVOCATIVE PRANK?

In the small town of Sevnica, a peculiar tribute to its most famous citizen has raised eyebrows. A life-size wooden statue of Melania Trump now stands overlooking the Sava River. In July 2019, a local artisan named Ales Zupevc—who goes by the nickname "Maxi"—used a chainsaw to carve a tree into a likeness of the US First Lady. With some added paint, he depicted her as she appeared on her husband's 2017 inauguration day, in her pale-blue Ralph Lauren coat, with one arm raised in a waving gesture.

Among the townspeople, not to mention the international media, the statue has had a decidedly mixed reception. Some admirers have praised its folksy charm, while critics have branded it a "scarecrow," a "Smurfette," and a "disgrace." Some observers have wondered if the whole thing is a joke.

The statue was commissioned by Brad Downey, a US artist known for pulling pranks. It's unclear if the outcome is what he had envisioned, but he told the media that he was happy with the result. The sculptor Maxi, for his part, is pleased with his work and hopes the real Melania Trump will see it someday.

SLAVIC ROOTS

Slovenes are a South Slavic ethnic group native to Slovenia, descended from Slavic peoples who settled the region between the Alps and the Adriatic Sea in the sixth century CE. They are also native to parts of Italy, Austria, and Hungary. Regardless of where today's national borders are drawn, ethnic Slovenes share a common ancestry, culture, and history, and many still speak Slovene as their native language.

NATIONAL IDENTITY

After the disintegration of Yugoslavia, interest in the concept of a distinct Slovene national identity grew. To that end, several historic and heraldic symbols were revived for use in national or nationalist insignia. This imagery, including an emblem of the three peaks of Mount Triglav, which is found in the nation's coat of arms, as well as the so-called Slovene Hat and the Black Panther—both symbols of the historic Slavic duchy, or territory, of Carantania—all function to create a sense of nationhood.

Slavic ethnicity is a large part of this identity, but not the only one. Cultural touchstones from myths and folktales, native flora and fauna, and beloved cultural heroes—the Romantic poet France Preseren (fran-SAY pre-SHEER-en), for example—all contribute to a sense of Slovene identity.

Members of a folklore group dance in a square in Ljubljana to celebrate a holiday.

GENDER EQUALITY

On average, the women of Slovenia are older than the men. Their median age is 46 years, as compared with 42.7 years for males. As is true in most countries, they tend to live longer than men, with an average life expectancy at birth of 84.2 years, compared with 78.3 years for males. The total fertility

US First Lady Melania Trump is one of the most famous modern figures from Slovenia.

rate in Slovenia is 1.58 children born per woman on average, which is relatively low. That figure put Slovenia at number 185 out of 224 countries, in which number 1 had the highest total fertility rate in the world, and number 224 had the lowest.

In terms of rights, gender equality is the law, but it remains a goal that has not been fully achieved. Still, compared with the other countries of the world, Slovenia is doing fairly well in its quest for gender equality. In 2019, the Organization for Economic Cooperation and Development (OECD) ranked Slovenia 8th out of 120 countries in its Social Institutions and Gender Index. This evaluation of gender-based discrimination rates the top country—in that year, Switzerland—as having the lowest degree of gender discrimination, and the bottom country, Yemen, as having the highest. Skewing the data was the fact that 60 countries could not be ranked for lack of sufficient data. Nevertheless, Slovenia's standing was impressive, well ahead of the United States, which ranked at number 26.

To arrive at the ranking in the index, the countries are evaluated according to a selection of indicators, including discrimination in the family, restricted physical integrity, restricted civil liberties, and restricted access to productive and financial resources. In Slovenia's case, the unequal burden of childcare, threat of domestic violence, and gender wage gap were among the issues seen as needing improvement.

One of the most famous Slovene women today is Melania Trump, who officially became the First Lady of the United States in 2017, when her husband, Donald Trump, became the US president. She was born Melanija Knavs in 1970 in Novo Mesto and grew up in the small town of Sevnica. At the time, Slovenia was a part of Yugoslavia. Many of the residents of Sevnica are proud of their hometown celebrity, and the association has brought more tourists to the town.

https://www.genderindex.org
This is the site for the OECD's Social Institutions and Gender Index.

https://www.newstatesman.com/world/europe/2017/12/slovenia-happy-country-should-be-even-happier
This article examines the general temperament of the Slovene people.

https://www.nytimes.com/2018/07/22/world/europe/melania-trump-sevnica-slovenia.html
This article explores how Melania Trump's hometown has responded to her fame.

http://www.slovenia25.si/i-feel-25/timeline/then-and-now/culture-as-the-basis-of-national-identity/index.html
This page provides a good explanation of how culture contributes to the Slovene identity.

http://www.slovenia25.si/symbols-of-slovenia/index.html
The country's symbols are discussed on this site.

https://www.stat.si/Popis2011/eng/default.aspx
The Republic of Slovenia Statistical Office reports demographic information.

https://www.theguardian.com/us-news/2019/jul/05/melania-trump-statue-slovenia-sevnica
This article on the wooden statue of Melania Trump includes several photos.

LIFESTYLE

A young family enjoys a summer picnic on the Big Pasture Plateau in the Kamnik-Savinja Alps.

7

THE PEOPLE OF SLOVENIA HAVE AN easygoing confidence in their country and their way of life. This confidence combines with pride in the country's great natural beauty and a healthy economy. Slovenes welcome visitors from other countries, and many families open their homes to tourists and business travelers.

From the 14th century until 1918, Slovenia was almost constantly under the rule of the Austro-Hungarian Empire. This history had a lasting influence on the Slovene way of life. The great flowering of Austrian culture, centered in Vienna in the 18th and 19th centuries, had a particularly strong impact on Slovenia's culture—its art, music, and theater—and even on foods and clothing styles. In western Slovenia, the proximity to Italy is evident in daily life. Some border towns, like Piran and Koper, are even bilingual, with signs and many documents in Italian as well as Slovene, even though only about 3,000 people of Italian descent live in Slovenia.

LIFE IN LJUBLJANA

Half of Slovenia's people live in cities, and the capital—Ljubljana—is by far the largest, with about 280,000 residents.

The pace of life in Ljubljana is slower and more relaxed than in cities in the United States or Western Europe. In addition, the city has a youthful aura, largely because of the presence of the University of Ljubljana. The

A city in Slovenia, as yet undetermined, will be named the European Capital of Culture for 2025. Since 1985, the EU has chosen one or more cities in EU member countries to carry the title for one year. During that time, the city organizes a series of events highlighting European culture and achievements. The Slovene cities vying for the honor are Lendava, Ljubljana, Nova Gorica, Kranj, and Ptuj.

university neighborhood is identified by the large numbers of bicycles and motor scooters, as well as the high percentage of people carrying laptops or wearing earbuds.

Ljubljana is a prosperous city, and most people have white-collar jobs in the many government offices, at the university, and with the many cultural institutions located there. Daily living patterns would seem quite familiar to most Americans. After a simple breakfast, kids rush off to school and adults take public transportation to work.

Evenings and weekends are a time for leisurely shopping in the many specialty shops or in the open-air produce market. Families and couples enjoy strolling through the narrow, winding streets of Old Town, where attractive old buildings are painted in soft pastel colors, and every turn presents a new scene straight out of a postcard. People also gravitate to Tivoli Park, where a popular recreation center offers swimming pools, tennis courts, bowling alleys, and a roller-skating rink.

Slovenes have a great fondness for concert music, opera, and dance. The major performance center, Cankarjev Dom (or the Cankar Center), has a schedule of nearly 700 events each year. Young people flock to a number of nightspots, featuring folk music, jazz, rock, and rap.

OTHER URBAN CENTERS

Slovenia's second-largest city is Maribor, located only a few miles from the Austrian border. The strong Austrian influence is evident in family meals, which are likely to include Austrian specialties, like *klobasa* (klo-BA-sa), or sausage, and *zavitek* (za-VEE-tek), or strudel, along with more traditional Slovene dishes, like the ever-present soup. This small city of less than 100,000 is more industrial than Ljubljana, so many men and women are employed in light industries. Maribor is also in the heart of Slovenia's wine-making region. Dozens of vineyards and wineries offer employment while also adding to the country's scenic beauty.

A few smaller cities are basically factory towns, like Jesenice, where about half the workers are employed in steel mills, and Kranj, a town of textile mills. Koper, a city of only 25,000 people, is Slovenia's major port. Life here is centered on the ports and tourist trade.

RURAL LIFE

Slovenia's population is almost evenly divided between urban and rural. The rural way of life shows a good deal of variety, depending in large part on location. In western Slovenia, for example, the villages of the Julian Alps are very much like the mountain villages of Italy and Switzerland. Farm families raise sheep, goats, and dairy cattle, while other villagers work in the large resort hotels and ski schools. Almost everyone in this region is a skier or hiker, or both.

Many rural families live in other resort areas. The town of Bled, for example, located on a spectacular glacial lake, is a world-famous resort, and the lives of the people there are geared to the tourist industry. Many open their homes to tourists and have been operating bed-and-breakfasts for several generations.

Slovenia is also well known for the healing properties of its springs. Spas have been attracting people from all over Europe since Roman times, and there are 15 major spas in operation today. Young people who are interested in alternative medicine and spa services often seek work at the spas or start massage parlors or beauty salons.

More traditional rural life is found throughout Slovenia's farm region, most of it in fertile river valleys. Many of the farms are run as cooperatives, a legacy of communist days, and this allows farm families to pool their resources for special needs like farm machinery.

In addition to wheat, corn, and other grains, farm families raise a variety of animals, including chickens, geese, sheep, goats, and dairy cattle. In addition, almost every farm has grapevines, both for the fruit and for wine making.

A resort spa in Rogaska Slatina features bathing pools and a beautiful setting in a region known for its mineral waters.

EDUCATION

Slovenia boasts one of the highest literacy rates in the world, with virtually everyone over the age of 10 able to read and write. Education is free and compulsory for all children between the ages of 6 and 14. More than half the student population now receives at least some education beyond high school.

Most Slovenes are fluent in at least one foreign language, and many people can speak and read two or three other languages. The most popular foreign languages are English, especially among young people; German (the language of Austria); Magyar (Hungarian); Italian; and Croatian.

Slovenia has four universities: the University of Ljubljana, the University of Maribor, the University of Primorska, and the University of Nova Gorica. The University of Ljubljana, founded in 1595, is considered one of the best in Europe. There are more than 30 other institutions of higher learning scattered throughout the country.

A Slovene elementary school student works on her lessons in the northwestern town of Ziri.

ALCOHOLISM

Alcoholism is a problem in Slovenia. In 2013, the country ranked fifth among European Union members in alcohol consumption, and studies incdicate that the numbers have increased since then. Not surprisingly, the numbers of deaths and illnesses from alcohol consumption are correspondingly high as well, according to the World Health Organization. Every day, alcohol is directly associated with two deaths in Slovenia, and road accidents caused by drunk drivers claim many lives every year.

To help combat that trend, in 2018 the National Institute of Public Health (NIJZ) launched the "SOPA" campaign, which is a Slovene acronym for "Together for Responsible Attitude to Alcohol." The project is training family doctors, nurses, and social workers to recognize and advise excessive drinkers. It targets people with risky drinking habits who have not yet developed alcoholism.

In Slovenia, drinking is a part of the culture. In the cities, workers like to start their day at a café with coffee, a bun, and a glass or two of *sadjevec* (SAD-yea-vetz), a liquor made from mixed fruits. In rural areas, there is a deep-rooted tradition of home brewing of wine, beer, and various liqueurs. Throughout the country, alcoholic beverages serve as a social bond—they are a part of celebrations and important events in life. Drinking, even excessively, is generally accepted by Slovene society, which poses problems for those trying to combat alcoholism.

THE COMMON GOOD

Despite its problems, there are many benefits to living in Slovenia. Programs for people's welfare are not merely government policy, they are part of the value system embraced by the Slovene people. In a popularly aggressive free-market economy, Slovenes treasure the unique programs of their social welfare state.

More than 25 percent of Slovenia's GDP is spent on social welfare. Roughly half of this goes to the pension and disability insurance system. The system provides social security for retired men over age 63 and retired women over age 61, with supplements for nonworking family members. It also covers people with disabilities who are unable to work and pays death benefits where indicated.

Health insurance is compulsory in Slovenia. It is overseen by the Institute of Health Insurance of Slovenia. All plan members are guaranteed access to health services, medicines and prescription drugs, technical aid, nursing services where necessary, and other costs. The Institute of Health Insurance contributes over 7 percent of the GDP annually to keep the program going. People can choose to supplement this insurance with private insurance if they wish, at their own cost.

Slovenia's health-care program provides free examinations for children, students, and pregnant women. Women are eligible for counseling concerning family planning, contraception, pregnancy, and childbirth. Under Slovenia's Family Income Act, they also receive cash compensation during maternity leave. Mothers—and fathers if necessary—are granted leave with pay for the purpose of childcare.

Under Slovenia's Civil Procedure Act, there is a system of free legal assistance for people in need, including defendants and claimants in lawsuits as well as defendants in criminal cases. All legal costs, including lawyers' fees and procedural charges, are covered.

Such measures provide a needed sense of security for Slovenes. Throughout their history, they have been ruled as a part of other nations—an empire, a patched-together monarchy, and a communist state—with different ethnic identities. In the truest sense, they are now a new nation.

INTERNET LINKS

https://www.cd-cc.si/en
The home site of the Cankarjev Dom shows the wide range of presentations held there.

http://www.slovenia.si
Various aspects of living in Slovenia are covered on this site.

https://welcomm-europe.eu/slovenia/welfare
This page lists the benefits of Slovenia's welfare programs.

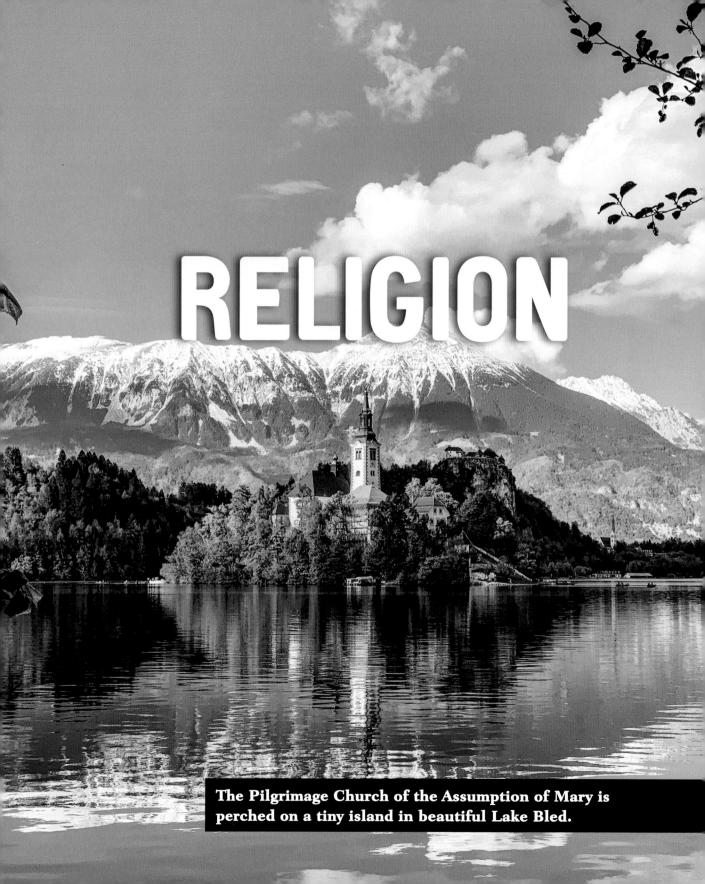

RELIGION

The Pilgrimage Church of the Assumption of Mary is perched on a tiny island in beautiful Lake Bled.

8

S LOVENIA HAS A GOOD REPUTATION for religious freedom and tolerance. The constitution guarantees freedom of religious practice and expression in private and in public. No person can be compelled to admit their religious or nonreligious beliefs. Though the great majority of Slovenes are Roman Catholic, there is no official state religion. Other faiths are practiced, and there is a significant portion of the population that does not follow any organized religion.

THE ROMAN CATHOLIC CHURCH

Historically, Catholicism has been a major influence on the culture of Slovenia. It is present in almost all Slovene art, literature, poetry, architecture, and crafts. Catholicism has become embedded in the national character and influences the everyday life of the people, even those who are non-Catholics or nonbelievers in any faith.

Determining the size of the country's Catholic population is problematic. The 2002 census reported about 57 percent of the people saying they were practicing Catholics. That is roughly 14 percent lower than the response in 1991, at the time that Slovenia was separating from communist Yugoslavia. In 2017, however, the Catholic Church itself reported that about 73 percent of Slovenes were Catholics. It's hard to know if the discrepancy in the figures shows an increase in the percentage of Catholics in the country or, more likely, a difference in methodology and interpretation. At the time of the 2002 census, for example, there was a widely publicized debate about whether it was acceptable for the government to ask highly personal questions, such as questions about one's religious practices. As a result, the census question about religion was not obligatory, which would easily skew the outcome. Another factor might be an interpretation of the term "practicing."

The 2002 census was the last year for which there is state data on religion in Slovenia. In 2011, the country conducted a register-based census, which did not provide any information on citizens' religious affiliation or ethnicity.

Regardless of the exact figures, it's certain that a majority of Slovenes are Roman Catholic. Like other Christians, Catholics worship a Holy Trinity made up of God, his son Jesus Christ, and the Holy Spirit. A belief in free

An interior view of Saint Martin's Parish Church in Bled shows the marble altars and frescoes painted in the 1930s.

will is key to Catholicism. Rituals of confession, repentance, and redemption play a large part in the faith. The priests and nuns who do the work of the church are required to take vows of celibacy. The head of the Roman Catholic Church is the pope, who is regarded as God's holy spokesman and whose declarations are considered infallible.

In Slovenia, as in other Roman Catholic nations, the Catholic Church stands firmly against contraception and abortion. Divorce is frowned upon. The Slovene Catholic Church has a patriarchal structure. Some people in Slovenia's urban areas view church doctrine as sexist. This may be one reason why the falloff in Catholic church attendance is greatest in the cities. Disillusionment with the church is greatest among intellectuals and members of the upper classes. Older people, particularly in rural areas, are offended by attempts to reform Catholicism and resentful of non-Latin masses and modernized services. They are among those that are sometimes drawn to the more emotional approach of the Evangelical Protestant churches.

The Franciscan Church of the Annunciation in Ljubljana dates from the 1600s and has been designated a cultural monument of national significance in Slovenia.

Despite a possible drop in membership, the Catholic Church still remains a power in Slovene daily life. It exerts an influence in government—though not officially—in schools, and in Slovene values.

NONBELIEVERS AND UNAFFILIATED

When queried about their religious affiliation in 2002, more than 300,000 (15.7 percent of Slovenes) refused to reply. While there may be other reasons, it is possible that many, if not most, of those who refused to state a religious preference were nonbelievers. Because of Slovenia's past role in communist Yugoslavia, where "state atheism" was urged on the people, a Slovene who today admits to not having a religious belief risks being labeled a communist.

Nevertheless, in addition to those who refused to answer, nearly 200,000 Slovenes (10.1 percent of the population) defined themselves as atheists, while about 300 defined themselves as agnostics. This makes atheists one of the largest groups in Slovenia, second only to Roman Catholics. Atheists don't believe that there is any higher power, while agnostics believe it is simply impossible to know if there is or is not a God or an afterlife. Some of these nonbelievers may be holdovers from the days of communism, but others seem to be rebelling against what they perceive to be the inflexible belief systems of all organized religions.

ISLAM

Islam has one of the two fastest-growing religions in Slovenia, with over 47,000 followers making up 2.4 percent of the population. (Since these figures date from 2002, however, that percentage is likely to be higher by now. In 2018, Muslim groups claimed there were 80,000 Muslims in Slovenia.) Muslims have been settling in Slovenia in increasing numbers over the past several decades, particularly since the outbreak of war in Bosnia and Kosovo. Both a new influx of Muslim refugees and a high birth rate have spurred an increase in the Muslim population of Slovenia.

The Islamic religion was founded by the Prophet Muhammad in 610 CE. Like Christianity and Judaism, it is a monotheistic religion, meaning that Muslims

believe in one God, whom they call Allah. Indeed, Islam acknowledges a common background among the three religions, embracing such biblical figures as Adam, Noah, Moses, and Jesus. For Muslims, Muhammad was the final in a series of prophets sent by God. Just as Christians and Jews live by Holy Scripture (the Bible or Torah), Muslims follow the Quran (sometimes spelled Koran), which articulates the rules for ethical and moral conduct in life.

In Slovenia, Muslims—as either new immigrants or refugees—tend to hold down the lowest-paying jobs, often doing work that native Slovenes do not wish to do. For many years, Muslims were not allowed to erect any mosques in Slovenia. All that changed in 2013, when the country's prime minister, Alenka Bratusek, formally laid the foundation stone for what would be Slovenia's first mosque. That was 44 years after the initial request to build it. At the ceremony, a Slovene official called the move "a symbolic victory against all forms of religious intolerance." Financed largely by the nation of Qatar, the Islamic Religious Cultural Center of Ljubljana was still under construction in 2019.

The Islamic Religious Cultural Center in Ljubljana is shown here while under construction.

The Church of Saints Cyril and Methodius in Ljubljana is an Eastern Orthodox church.

THE EASTERN ORTHODOX CHURCH

The Eastern Orthodox Christians of Slovenia are almost as numerous as the Muslims, with a total of over 45,000 believers, or 2.3 percent of the population. (Again, these figures are from 2002, the last time a census was administered. A 2018 European Commission report provides a statistic of 3.7 percent for both Muslims and Eastern Orthodox Christians.) The Eastern Orthodox Church is distinct from the Roman Catholic Church. The faithful follow different rites from those of Roman Catholicism and do not recognize the pope as their leader.

Although the rites of Eastern Orthodox Christians tend to be more elaborate than those of Roman Catholics, in other respects the Eastern religion is more relaxed. For instance, clergy are permitted to marry and have children. Divorce and remarriage are not condemned, but a remarriage ceremony must include prayer and repentance for the sin of divorce. The Eastern Orthodox community in Slovenia includes a large number of Serbs who migrated there in search of work or in flight from Croat repression. Many of them are former officers and soldiers of what was the Yugoslav army. They have settled mostly in urban areas.

OTHER FAITHS

Fewer than 20,000 Slovenes (less than 1 percent of the population) follow other religions than those discussed above. The largest of these groups are Evangelicals, with some 14,000 members. Each of the other religious groups—including non-Evangelical Protestants, Buddhists, Hindus, various minor sects, and Jews (in 2016, there were an estimated 100 to 300 Jews in Slovenia)—account for 0.1 percent or less of the Slovene population.

The Ursuline Church of the Holy Trinity in Ljubljana is an unusual baroque structure dating from 1726.

HOLY SITES

The religious buildings of Slovenia provide visible evidence of the effect of faith on the tradition and culture of the people. Many of these structures are centuries old and are maintained as national treasures. Others have been lovingly restored. Among the most notable is the Ursuline Church of the Holy Trinity in the center of Ljubljana, which was built in 1726. It is famous for a beautiful multicolored altar made of African marble.

The Cathedral of the Assumption is on the city square in the seaport of Koper. Most of the structure dates from the 18th century, but some of it has been retained from buildings of earlier times. The cathedral tower, known as City Tower, dates back to the 14th century. The top is reached by a long staircase, and the view is spectacular. The interior of the cathedral is richly decorated

An aerial view of the Kostanjevica Monastery shows its large central courtyard. The monastery is no longer in operation, and the building is now a site devoted to arts and cultural events.

with marble columns and religious paintings. The cathedral also contains the sarcophagus, or tomb, of Saint Nazarius, the patron saint of the city.

Kostanjevica Monastery, with the Church of the Annunciation of Our Lady, stands on Kostanjevica Hill in Nova Gorica. The hill rises 469 feet (143 m) above the border with Italy, and there is a sweeping view of the countryside valleys from the church. Attached to the church is a 17th-century Franciscan monastery containing many treasures from the past. The last members of the 19th-century French royal family, the Bourbons, are buried in a crypt beneath the church.

The Church of the Holy Trinity in the mining town of Idrija was built in 1500. Legend has it that the church was built atop a mercury mine discovered by a local tub maker. The mine, one of the largest of its kind in the world, was the reason that the city of Idrija grew up around it.

The Novo Mesto Cathedral is said to "rise above the town like a swan." Also called Saint Nicholas's Cathedral, the church dates back to 1493 and is famous for its altar image of Saint Nicholas by the noted Italian painter Tintoretto.

The Maribor Synagogue, in Maribor, Slovenia, dates to medieval times—possibly as early as the 13th century. In 2015, it was granted status as a cultural landmark of national importance. The building is one of the few surviving medieval synagogues in Europe. In 1501, after the expulsion of the Jews from Maribor, it was converted into a church, and over the centuries, the red-roofed building has played more mundane roles. The synagogue was restored in the 1990s and opened in 2001 as a Jewish Heritage Center, with a memorial to the victims of the Holocaust. It is one of two historic synagogue buildings that stand today in Slovenia; the other is a 19th-century synagogue in Lendava, now used as a museum and culture center.

This is only a sampling of the rich religious architecture of Slovenia. The country is dotted with remarkable buildings, large and small, demonstrating the role that faith has played in Slovenia's history.

INTERNET LINKS

https://religious-freedom-report.org/report/?report=835
An overview of religious freedom and tolerance in Slovenia is provided on this site.

https://www.slovenia.info/en/things-to-do/culture/churches -and-monasteries
This site has beautiful pictures of some of the religious buildings in Slovenia.

LANGUAGE

A milk vending machine at a farmers' market in Ljubljana shows signs written in Slovene.

9

SLOVENE IS THE LANGUAGE OF Slovenia. It is a South Slavic language spoken by around 2.5 million people worldwide. Most of them, naturally, reside in Slovenia, but some speakers live in border regions of Italy, Austria, Hungary, Serbia, and Croatia. Also, the language can be heard in certain communities of expatriate Slovenes in Europe, the United States, Canada, Argentina, Australia, and South Africa. Written in the Roman alphabet, the words are closely related to Croatian and Serbian words, but not interchangeable with them. Slovene grammar is extremely complicated and has many cases, genders, and tenses.

Like most European languages, aside from modern English, Slovene has a T-V distinction. There are two forms of "you"—one informal and one formal. Informal "you" (*ti* form in Slovene) is singular and is used with family or close friends, or when speaking to children. Formal "you" (*vi* form) is plural and is used in polite conversation, formal situations,

Slovene is one of the only Indo-European languages that uses what is called "dual." That is a grammatical number in addition to singular and plural. Dual is used when referring to precisely two persons, objects, or concepts. Although English has lost the dual forms it once had, it still retains residual traces of it, such as in the dual "both" and "couple."

or when addressing a superior. (In English, the informal, or familiar, T form of "you" was "thou," which has disappeared from modern usage.)

GERMANIZATION

Through much of the country's history, Slovene was a secondary language kept alive by determined scholars like the author Primoz Trubar, the grammarian Anton Janezic, and others. During the 600 years Slovenia was ruled by the Austro-Hungarian Empire, the German language was imposed on the population, and Slovene was looked down upon as a dialect spoken mostly by peasants. With the Nazi occupation of World War II, German, as well as Italian in some sections of the country, was insisted upon by the occupying forces.

There has been, to a significant extent, a Germanization of the Slovene language. Many German words and phrases have made their way into conversational use. Most of them, over time, have been distorted into what Slovenes regard as their own words and phrases, but their origins are unmistakable. The German influence is particularly evident when it comes to slang or colloquial speech.

ALPHABET AND DIALECT

The Slovene alphabet has 25 letters. Five of the letters are vowels, and 20 are consonants. There is no *q, w, x,* or *y*. However, there are two versions of *c*, two versions of *s*, and two versions of *z*. The words that are formed often string consonants together in ways that seem unnatural to non-Slovene eyes and ears.

According to an old saying, if you don't have a dialect, you don't have a language. There are many dialects in the Slovene language. (The exact number is difficult to determine, as speech patterns overlap and the point where one dialect becomes another is something linguists debate.) They vary from region to region, with a *vzhodno* (wsh-OD-no) dialect spoken in eastern Slovenia, a *zahadno* (za-HOD-no) patois prevailing in the west, an *osrednje* (o-SRED-nee) slang used in the central region, and a *primorsko* (pree-MORE-sko) dialect favored in the areas near the Adriatic seacoast. Dialect speakers use the same

Primoz Trubar is hailed as the father of Slovene literature. He was a scholar who turned the Slovene dialect into a structured language, and who wrote the first books in Slovene.

Trubar was born in the village of Rasica in Slovenia on June 9, 1508. His parents were religious Roman Catholics, and a deep commitment to God was instilled in him as a child. He attended school in Rijeka from 1522 to 1524, and he then went to Salzburg, Austria, to continue his education.

From Salzburg, he went to Trieste, Italy, to further his religious experience. He came under the influence of Bishop Pietro Bonomo, a member of the emerging humanist movement. The young Trubar mingled with humanist writers and was swayed by their views. In particular, he became a disciple of Erasmus, who is considered by many historians to be one of the greatest philosophical thinkers of his time.

Having enrolled at the University of Vienna in 1528 to further both his religious and philosophical studies, Trubar left after two years. His time there, however, had deepened his religious commitment, and so he returned to Slovenia and became a preacher. Under the humanist influence, he began leaning away from the Roman Catholic faith and toward Protestantism.

In 1547, labeled a heretic, Trubar was expelled from Slovenia. He went to Rothenberg, Germany, to preach as a Protestant minister. There he wrote Catechismus *(in 1550), a catechism, and* Abecedarium *(in 1555), an alphabet primer. They were the first books ever written in the Slovene language.* Catechismus *was published in 1550 in Tubingen, Germany. He produced 20 more books in Slovene during the years that followed. The most important is a Slovene translation of the New Testament.*

Trubar died in Derendingen, Germany, on June 28, 1586. He was 78 years old. In 2008, the 500th anniversary of the year of Trubar's birth, the government of Slovenia proclaimed the Year of Primoz Trubar. Since 2010, Slovenia has recognized June 8 as Primoz Trubar Day. In 2013, Google celebrated Trubar's 505th birthday with a dedicated Google Doodle.

Brizinski Spomeniki *is the Slovene name for the Freising Manuscripts, the oldest written texts in the Slovene language. They consist of three sermons on sin and repentance and are believed to have been written by Bishop Abraham of Slovenia between 957 and 994 CE. Four parchment leaves and a quarter of a page have been preserved.*

Bishop Abraham owned, and at times lived on, a large estate in central Slovenia. He also served the Roman Catholic Church in Freising, Germany, where he is believed to have written the manuscripts. The bishop died over 1,000 years ago on May 26, 994.

In 1807, papers from the Freising Diocese were transferred to the Munich National Library to be examined. It was during the examination that the Freising Manuscripts were discovered.

The Slovene Academy of Sciences and Arts published a facsimile of the Freising Manuscripts in 1992 and made it available for public viewing. In 1994, the Bank of Slovenia issued three limited edition coins—one gold, one silver, and one made of a copper-zinc alloy—to commemorate the Freising Manuscripts. Imprinted on these coins, using the original Latin script, are the words glagolite ponaz—*the Slovene words with which the first Freising Manuscript begins. Roughly translated, it means "speak our language."*

Slovene language but often arrange sentences and pronounce words in very different ways. It's similar to the difference between the speech of Appalachia and that of New York City, or between the French of rural Quebec and that of Paris.

The manner of speaking can be as important as the words in Slovene conversation. A certain formality prevails when city people address one another. In rural areas, speech is apt to be guarded, and body language takes on added importance. In both city and countryside, politeness and good manners prevail.

SECOND LANGUAGES

Most Slovenes speak a second language. The most common one is German. Italian, Croatian, and Serbian are also understood and spoken in different parts of the country. In the major cities, English is fast becoming the second language of choice. This is particularly true among young people, as American films, music, and clothing are being assimilated into the culture. American slang, in particular, may be heard in the streets of Ljubljana and other major cities.

INTERNET LINKS

http://nl.ijs.si/e-zrc/bs/index-en.html
This scholarly site offers information about the Freising Manuscripts, including an English translation at this link: http://nl.ijs.si/e-zrc/bs/html/bsTR.html#bsTR-eng.

https://www.omniglot.com/writing/slovene.htm
This site offers an introduction to Slovene and offers audio files for many common phrases.

http://www.trubar2008.gov.si/eng/trubarjevo_leto/uvod/index.html
The Slovene "Year of Trubar" site is available in English.

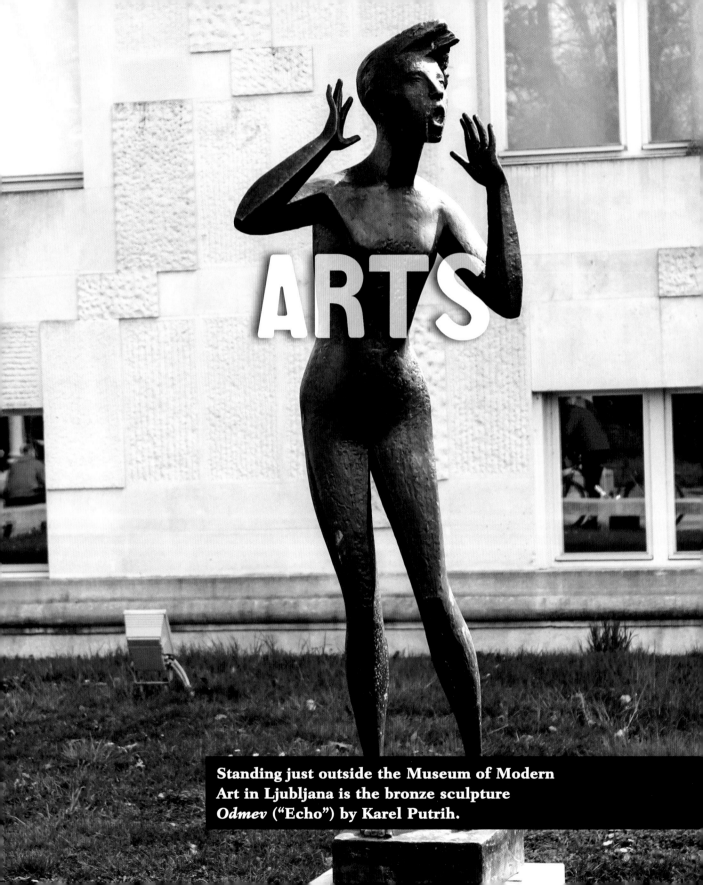

ARTS

Standing just outside the Museum of Modern Art in Ljubljana is the bronze sculpture *Odmev* ("Echo") by Karel Putrih.

10

THE SLOVENE PEOPLE GREATLY value the arts. This can be seen in the many exhibitions, events, festivals, and performances that crowd the calendar each year. Ljubljana has a lively arts scene, and in many ways the country's capital city is itself a tribute to Slovene arts and culture. From folk arts to cutting-edge contemporary works, Slovene writers, artists, and musicians explore, interpret, and create their world. They play a major role in the emerging consciousness of this relatively new nation.

LITERATURE

Poetry prevails in the literary tradition of Slovenia. France Preseren, the most famous and beloved Slovene poet, established a romantic and nationalistic tradition for the Slovene poets who followed him. Long after Preseren's death, Tomaz Salamun's poem "Eclipse" was still bitterly lamenting the absence of Slovene nationhood and proclaiming that "I grew tired of the image of my tribe and moved out." Preseren's romantic

The National Gallery of Slovenia is the principal art museum in Slovenia. Located in Ljubljana, it holds the country's largest collection of fine art from the late medieval period through the 20th century. When the city's Museum of Modern Art opened in 1947, many of the National Gallery's 20th-century pieces were transferred there. Today, among works by more than 1,000 artists, the National Gallery holds a collection of 97 pieces by the Slovene artist Zoran Music.

despair lives on in the poetic reflection on doomed love by Uros Zupan, which asks, "And what is left? A quiet room, the smell of the carpet which will fill the room long after we have each gone our own way."

The new young poets of Slovenia carry on this tradition with works that reflect both the bittersweet romantic and idealistically nationalist influences of Preseren's verses. In 2019, for example, the winner of the annual Preseren Award was the 42-year-old poet Jure Jakob, who takes his motifs mostly from nature. Growing up in rural Slovenia, he says, influenced his poetry. "I walk in the woods more often than in the galleries. That's why a blackbird or an ant will find its way into my poem sooner than a car or a cyclist."

Among novelists, the writer, playwright, and essayist Drago Jancar is one of the most esteemed, widely read, and translated Slovene writers. His many novels include *In Ljubezen Tudi* (*And Love Itself*), published in 2017.

Books are for sale for 1 euro apiece at a flea market in Ljubljana.

The life, legend, and poetry of France Preseren are in many ways a reflection of the Slovene national character. His romanticism, pessimism, and lyrical flights of fancy echo both the history, myths, and artistic patterns of the nation. He is considered the father of modern Slovene literature.

Preseren was born on December 3, 1800, in Vrba, Slovenia. At that time, Slovenia was part of the Austro-Hungarian Empire and was benefiting from educational reforms instituted by Empress Maria Theresa. These reforms had increased literacy and created a reading public hungry for more works in their native language. France Preseren was destined to satisfy that hunger.

As a boy, France went to live with an uncle in Kopanje. He went to elementary school there and returned home only during holidays. When he was 21 years old, he went to Vienna, where he studied law. There, he was influenced by the romantic movement in European literature. When he returned to Slovenia as a civil servant and lawyer, he began writing poetry. Life during this period was a struggle for him; his work was tedious, and the pay was barely enough to sustain him.

Preseren was described as gentle, good-hearted, romantic, and freethinking. During the 1830s, he fell hopelessly in love and suffered a painful rejection, and in 1835, his closest friend, Matija Cop, drowned while swimming in the Sava River. Preseren became deeply depressed. He had wavy black hair and deep gray eyes, an image that fit the soulful feelings some of his poetry evoked.

His unhappy love affair inspired Sonetni Venec (A Wreath of Sonnets), which reflects not just his personal misery but the national consciousness of a subjugated people. The epic poem Krst pri Savici (The Baptism on the Savica), which was dedicated to Matija Cop, illustrates a peculiarly Slovene combination of such traits as patriotism, pessimism, and resignation. "Zdravljica" ("A Toast"), by Preseren, encompasses the Slovene yearning for independence and peace. The seventh stanza, set to the music of Stanko Premrl, was adopted as the country's national anthem. It reflects a pacifist sentiment, which is unusual among nationalistic songs.

France Preseren died on February 8, 1849, not yet 50 years old. The themes and structure of his work set the standards for the Slovene poets who followed. His poems are taught in the schools, and he is recognized throughout the land as "the greatest Slovene poet."

Goran Vojnovic (b. 1980) is perhaps today's best-known Slovene writer. The novelist, poet, screenwriter, and film director achieved fame for his 2008 novel, *Cefurji Raus!* ("*Southern Scum Go Home!*"), which deals with unwanted immigrants in Slovenia. The title is a reference to a popular graffiti slogan seen on the streets of Ljubljana. For this novel, Vojnovic was awarded the prestigious Preseren Award. Vojnovic's most recent movel, *Figa* (*The Fig*) has not yet been published in English as of 2019.

THEATER

Theater is a major part of Slovenia's national culture. The nation's first professional theater was founded in the 18th century in Ljubljana, when Slovenia was still part of the Austro-Hungarian Empire. Today, there is a Slovene National Theater in both Ljubljana and Maribor. There are other theaters, including

The Ljubljana Opera House is the home of the Slovene National Theater Opera and Ballet Ljubljana company.

puppet theaters for children, in cities and towns throughout Slovenia. On average, about 100 professional productions take place each year.

FILM

Though it doesn't typically gain a great deal of notice internationally, Slovenia's filmmaking industry has been producing movies for decades. Some have stood out over the years. The film *History of Love* by Sonja Prosenc was Slovenia's submission to the 2020 Academy Awards as its candidate for consideration in the Best International Feature Film category. The movie is about a 17-year-old girl, Iva, who is in the process of coming to terms with the death of her mother.

In addition to its homegrown films, the country is hoping to attract more international moviemakers to shoot films in Slovenia. To that end, the Slovenian Film Center and the Ministry of Culture have been presenting attractive

A street banner publicizes a film festival called "Under the Stars" in Ljubljana.

One of the most acclaimed Slovene artists is the painter and printmaker Zoran Music (1909–2005). Born in Bukovica, he studied art in Zagreb, Croatia, and traveled widely. In 1944, while World War II was raging, he was arrested by the Nazi forces. Suspected of being an antifascist spy, he was sent to the notorious Dachau concentration camp in Germany. There he made more than 150 sketches of the brutality of life in the camp. After liberation, he managed to save around 100 of the drawings—including dreadful images of suffering people, piles of corpses, hanged men, and cremation ovens. From his experience at Dachau, he went on to create his most acclaimed series of paintings, We Are Not the Last, *in the 1970s.*

All of Music's work did not focus on Nazi atrocities, however. He also created landscapes and portraits in a variety of styles. After 1952, he lived and worked mostly in Paris and Venice and became well known among art circles. In addition to numerous prestigious international awards, he was recognized in Slovenia in 1991, when he was presented the Preseren Award for lifetime achievement. Today, the National Gallery of Slovenia holds a large collection of his pieces, and his works are also found in museums and galleries worldwide.

productions at the Cannes Film Festival and other venues publicizing the country's wide array of geographical settings. Slovenia is also offering cash rebates to foreign filmmakers.

PAINTING

Slovene painting traditions have deep roots. During the Renaissance and the overlapping baroque period, between roughly the 13th and 17th centuries, Slovene painters and sculptors were influenced by art movements originating in Italy and, to a lesser extent, the Austro-Hungarian Empire.

Beautiful paintings with mostly mythic and religious themes rendered by Slovene artists can be viewed in many of the nation's churches, castles, and galleries. Included are works by baroque painters Giulio Quaglio, Franc Jelovsek, Johann Caspar Waginger, and Anton Lerchinger. Several works by the best-known Slovene painter of the period, Valentin Janez Metzinger, are hung in the Novo Mesto Cathedral.

The life of baroque painter Anton Cebej is shrouded in mystery. Neither his date of birth nor the date of his death are known. It is believed that he came from Sturje, in the Vipava region of Slovenia, and that he painted between 1750 and 1774. He was influenced by the baroque Venetian painters, but his work has a Central European intensity. Three of his paintings—*Corpus Christi*, *Saint Leopold*, and *Saint Florian*— hang in the National Gallery in Ljubljana. They are characterized by brilliant colors and bold compositions.

During the romantic movement in art (in the late 18th to mid-19th century), the landscape art of Anton Karinger flourished in Slovenia. He was followed by Ivana Kobilca, Slovenia's best-known female painter, who produced most of her 200 oil paintings during the 1880s. Her work, which hangs in art galleries throughout Europe, illustrates the crossover from the realism that replaced romanticism to the impressionist school, which would begin to flower around the turn of the 20th century. During that period, Ivan Grohar also made the transition from realism to impressionism with paintings of Slovene landscapes and peasant life.

Saint Leopold is one of Anton Cebej's most notable paintings.

Impressionism evolved into a more abstract expressionist style in Slovenia following World War I. From the 1920s through the 1950s, Franz Kralj and Veno Pilon were the leading Slovene expressionist artists. Kralj's paintings, along with his woodcuts and sculptures, may be viewed at the Museum of Modern Art in Ljubljana. Much of Pilon's work, including both paintings and

A NEANDERTHAL FLUTE?

Slovenia lays claim to the world's oldest musical instrument yet discovered, a flute dating from up to 60,000 years ago. The "Neanderthal flute"—a controversial designation—is displayed at the National Museum of Slovenia in Ljubljana. The Slovene archaeologist Ivan Turk found it in 1995 at the Divje Babe excavation site, a cave overlooking the Idrijca River near Cerkno. Over the years, numerous artifacts from the Paleolithic era have been discovered there.

The "flute" is a 5-inch (12-centimeter) thigh-bone fragment from a young cave bear. It appears to have had two to five holes carved or drilled into it, and a replica has proved that it can make music. However, not only do archaeologists disagree on which species of early human might have made it, they differ on whether it was human-made at all. Some archaeologists suggest the holes in the bone were chewed by a carnivore. Either way, the bone may—or may not—have been used as a musical instrument.

Scientists favoring the theory that it was human- or Neanderthal-made (whether or not Neanderthals were humans, or were capable of making music, is yet another controversial topic) point out that the holes are spaced apart precisely in a way not seen in other animal-chewed bones. The holes form musical notes when breath is blown through one end of the bone. The notes are different when the holes are covered and uncovered in a variety of arrangements that point to the making of music rather than mere noise.

However, a 2015 article published in the science journal Royal Society *asserts the idea of a Paleolithic flute is merely wishful thinking. Such "instruments," it says, are merely the result of hyenas chewing up bear cubs in cave bear dens.*

Not only that, but some experts are now saying the actual oldest known musical instruments are bone flutes found in 2012 in southern Germany. Made around 42,000 to 43,000 years ago, they were indisputably made by Homo sapiens, *or modern humans. Some researchers suggest that the ability to make music may have been one of the intellectual and behavioral advantages that gave modern humans a survival edge over other—now extinct—human or prehuman species. In other words, Neanderthals did not make flutes because they had no concept of music.*

Singers dressed in traditional costumes perform Slovene folk songs.

photographic studies, has a more surrealist style and can be seen in the Pilon Galerie in the Slovene town of Ajdovscina, where he was born.

Singers dressed in traditional costumes perform Slovene folk songs.

MUSIC

Slovene music dates back to the 16th century. That was when Jacobus Gallus Carniolus (1550—1591), also known as Jacobus Gallus or Jakob Petelin, wrote his first sacred compositions. A monk from Ribnica, Carniolus's most notable work is the six-part *Opus Musicum* designed as a series to go along with the church's annual worship program. Written for eight voices, the *Opus Musicum*

Ljubljana, the capital of Slovenia, was virtually remade by the vision of architect Joze Plecnik (YOH-zha PLAYCH-nik). The parks and squares; the library, museum, and government buildings; the stadium; the bridges; and even the banks of the Ljubljanica River are all the result of Plecnik's 15-year project to redesign the city. Viewed as a whole, the Ljubljana of Plecnik is a testament to his theory that architecture must express the history of its setting through careful research. He advocated building to a human scale, by which he meant that the eventual user of the architecture must be taken into consideration along with history and setting when planning a structure.

Joze Plecnik was born on January 23, 1872, in Ljubljana. In the 1890s, he went to Vienna, where he met Otto Wagner, author of the highly influential book Modern Architecture. Plecnik enrolled in the architecture department of the Academy of Fine Arts and studied under Wagner for three years. In 1921, Plecnik returned to Ljubljana as head of the architecture department at the new Ljubljana University. World War I had freed Slovenia from Austro-Hungarian rule, and there was a movement to express a national identity and culture through art, literature, and architecture. Plecnik was charged not only with educating the first generation of Slovene architects but also with redesigning the nation's capital. He worked until World War II broke out. During that period, his architecture established a Slovene identity for the city.

The Triple Bridge connects the Old Town to the modern city on the other side of the river.

One of his most memorable works is the famous Triple Bridge across the Ljubljanica River. Plecnik resumed his work after the war.

In 1956, he died at age 84. His memorial is Ljubljana itself, a city of architectural images that epitomize the culture of Slovenia.

contrasts with some of the other music that he wrote, including both rhythmic, madrigal-style melodies and a still much-performed funeral anthem titled *The Ways of Zion Do Mourn*.

By 1701, the Slovene public's taste had shifted from church music to embrace the baroque compositions of the period, and the Slovenian Philharmonic Society was founded. Over the succeeding years, its honorary members would include composers Ludwig van Beethoven, Niccolo Paganini, and Johannes Brahms. Subsequently, famed Austrian composer Gustav Mahler was musical conductor of the Ljubljana Provincial Theater from 1881 to 1882, early in his career.

The Slovenian Philharmonic Hall dates to 1891, but the music society itself began in 1701.

Perhaps Slovenia's best-loved composer is Hugo Wolf (1860—1903). He composed many *lieder*, or art songs, based on the works of great romantic poets like Eduard Morike and Johann Wolfgang von Goethe. These, along with a series of Spanish and Italian songs, are a major part of the Slovene folk song heritage. He also wrote an opera, *Der Corregidor* (1890), which was unsuccessful, as were several of his symphonic pieces. It was only when he used folktales and poetry as inspiration that his music truly flowered.

Slovene music today is varied. The Ljubljana String Quartet regularly performs classical pieces on concert stages throughout Slovenia and abroad. The musical group Terrafolk includes classical, pop, and rock in its repertoire and jazzes up Romany, Irish, Klezmer, Mexican, and Slovene music. Winners of the World Music 2003 Audience Award, the group teamed up with the European Symbolic Orchestra in 2016 to release the album *XXLive*. The female vocal folk group Katice, with its multiple harmonic voices, is also popular. Slovenia also has artists and bands in every imaginable category, from punk rock to heavy metal to hip-hop and beyond. Among the newcomers, the indie electro duo zalagasper (Zala Kralj and Gasper Santl) represented Slovenia in the 2019 Eurovision Song Contest to great acclaim.

DANCE

Folk dancing is festive in Slovenia, and colorful peasant costumes are often worn, particularly in the smaller towns. The dances themselves, while heavily influenced by the long Austro-Hungarian rule, also incorporate movements from Ukraine, Russia, Italy, and Serbia. The result is a melding of forms combining traditional movements with innovative techniques that can only be described as uniquely Slovene.

There is also a tradition of ballet in Slovenia, which dates back to the 18th-century cultural programs of the Austrian empress Maria Theresa. Today, ballet is part of the national culture. Among the more prominent ballet companies are the innovative Fico Balet and the National Ballet.

Folklore enthusiasts dance in the city square in Ljubljana.

https://www.dailyartmagazine.com/ivana-kobilca-slovenia
A vivid portrait of painter Ivana Kobilca and her art is offered in this article.

https://www.ficobalet.org
The Fico Balet site presents a video of an amusing soccer ballet.

https://www.independent.co.uk/arts-entertainment/music/features/whos-afraid-of-hugo-wolf-124536.html
This article is about the intense, short life of Hugo Wolf.

https://www.independent.co.uk/news/obituaries/zoran-music-295277.html
This obituary for Zoran Music provides an overview of his life and work.

https://www.ng-slo.si/en
The National Gallery of Slovenia site offers a wealth of images of its permanent collection, organized by time period.

https://www.nms.si/en/collections/highlights/343-Neanderthal -flute
The National Museum of Slovenia's page about the controversial Neanderthal flute expresses no doubts about its origins.

https://theculturetrip.com/europe/slovenia/articles/up-and -coming-slovenian-bands-you-need-to-know
Some of Slovenia's newer music groups are profiled in this article.

https://www.visitljubljana.com/en/visitors/explore/things-to-do/ art-and-culture/article/10-masterpieces-by-joze-plecnik
A slide show presents the works of Joze Plecnik.

LEISURE

Two women scale a steep, rocky hillside above the village of Mojstrana.

11

S LOVENES ARE VIGOROUS FOLKS, and their leisure-time activities reflect this. They take to the outdoors for their recreation in both summer and winter. Their alpine terrain gives them plenty of opportunities for skiing, hiking, and mountain climbing, and the many rivers provide recreational destinations for swimming, rafting, and kayaking. Slovenes live close to nature and relax in harmony with it.

WINTER SPORTS

Skiing is by far the most popular sport in Slovenia. One out of every four Slovenes is an active skier. Slovenes take pride in the sport. Their proudest moment came on October 7, 2000. That was the day that Davo Karnicar skied nonstop down Mount Everest, the world's highest mountain. He was the first person to ever descend from the 29,035-foot (8,850 m) crest of the mountain on skis.

From December to March, the well-equipped ski resorts in the Julian Alps are booked to capacity. The most popular area is the Kranjska Gora winter sports center in the northwest corner of Slovenia, bordering Austria

A climb up Mount Triglav in the Julian Alps is a must for a Slovene mountain climber. Depending on the route, an ascent takes most people two days, and can take anywhere from 7 to 19 hours of climbing. There are several mountain huts along the way where weary climbers can spend the night. Only the most experienced, fit climbers can reach the summit in one day.

and Italy. Overlooking Triglav National Park, Kranjska Gora is famous for the championship events and ski-jumping contests held there. Its Pianica ski jump is the world's first such site over 656 feet (200 m) high.

Vacationing Slovenes also go downhill sleigh riding at night on the torch-lit slopes of Kranjska Gora. During days when the ski runs can get overcrowded, the more adventurous climb the area's frozen waterfalls, using ice picks to grasp the ice. Those seeking less strenuous pleasures go ice-skating on nearby Lake Bled, surrounded by dense pine forests and towered over by the snowcapped Julian Alps.

MOUNTAIN CLIMBING

Mountain climbing and rock climbing in the alpine regions of Slovenia can be dangerous pastimes. Many Slovenes in the hilly parts of the country are natural climbers. Others take to it as a challenge.

The ultimate challenge for Slovene climber Tomaz Humar back in November 1999 was Dhaulagiri Mountain in north-central Nepal. His solitary climb up

A climber takes in the view from the peak of **Triglav Mountain.**

the 13,125-foot (4,000 m) south face of Dhaulagiri was—in the words of a rival climber—crossing "the boundary of the impossible" into a "death zone." Humar's success made him a national hero and inspired a generation of Slovenes to take up mountain climbing. His 2009 death during another solo climb in the Himalayas was a loss for the nation.

SUMMERTIME ACTIVITIES

Slovenia's 29-mile (47 km) shoreline on the Adriatric Sea offers some of the best ocean swimming and snorkeling in Europe. Three of the beaches received the European Union Blue Flag in recognition of their ecological soundness and upkeep. Not just Slovenes but vacationers from all over Europe flock to the clean and inexpensive hotels along these beaches in the warm weather. There are also private apartments available that provide changes of linen and cleaning services. These are very popular with Slovene students, who pool their money and sometimes arrange seasonal shares with staggered visits for as many as a dozen or more occupants.

Lake Bled offers swimmers a cool dip in clear mountain water.

Mountain bikers ride down the trail at Bike Park Pohorje in Maribor.

There are many other warm-weather activities available for older children in Slovenia. Summer camps, often located alongside one or another of the country's many lakes, offer a wide variety of programs. Some feature conventional sports, water sports, crafts, and nature studies, while others specialize in specific disciplines. There are karate camps, soccer camps, computer camps, and camps devoted to gymnastics.

Both older children and young adults enroll in the ever-popular biking tours routed over various regions of the country. They cover areas from the Julian Alps to the Skocjan Caves, from the Adriatic Sea to the capital city of Ljubljana, and from the valleys of Slovenj Gradec to the artificial lakes of Podravje. Some of these bike tours are combined with nature studies. One of them is devoted to the capture and identification of the many different and beautiful species of butterflies in Slovenia.

HIKERS AND BOATERS

Cycling and other strenuous outdoor activities are not limited to summertime. Spring and fall are also active periods for the many Slovenes who prefer to take their vacations before or after the summer influx of tourists. Hiking the alpine trails or the forests of Koroska is pleasant in milder weather. Swimming alongside schools of trout in the crystal-clear waters of Lake Bohinj is only possible when the vacation crowds have thinned out.

Autumn and spring are also the seasons favored by boaters in Slovenia for exploring the coves and inlets of Slovenia's many lakes in kayaks and canoes. Braver kayakers will follow the white-water rafters into the rushing streams of the Soca, Mislinja, Kolpa, or Sava Rivers. Some rafters will explore the underground rivers in the caves of southwest Slovenia. These sites also attract many spelunkers (cave explorers). Because of the unusual nature of the Slovene cave complexes and the many fascinating specimens of both flora and fauna to be found there, spelunking has become an increasingly popular leisure activity for Slovenes.

On Lake Bled, a man paddles in a kayak before the impressive backdrop of Bled Castle and the snow-covered Julian Alps.

TEAMS AND SPECTATORS

Competitive sports are popular with players and spectators. Many young people, both male and female, join soccer teams that compete against each other in local leagues. Soccer, called football in Slovenia, is a spectator sport that draws large crowds. Fans are loyal and vocal, and they support their teams strongly. Stozice Stadium, the main venue for the national team, is located in Ljubljana and has a capacity of more than 16,000 seats. Curiously, the Slovene team doesn't have a nickname,

Slovenia (*in blue and white*) and Latvia battle it out at a UEFA Euro 2020 qualification tournament in Riga, Latvia, in June 2019. Slovenia won this game but ultimately failed to qualify for the finals.

like most other national teams have. Efforts to choose or assign one have so far fallen flat.

Basketball is also a big sport, with both a men's and women's national team. They have qualified to compete at Eurobasket, the European Basketball Championship. In 2017, the men's team won its first-ever tournament championship. Meanwhile, the women's team qualified for Eurobasket for the first time that same year and competed in it again in 2019. After helping his team win the 2017 Eurobasket title, star player Luka Doncic went on to play professionally in the United States. He joined the Dallas Mavericks, where he was named NBA Rookie of the Year for the 2018 to 2019 season.

WOMEN COMPETITORS

Slovene women excel in all sorts of activities. From the time they are very small, Slovene children are encouraged to exercise. Gymnastics becomes part of the leisure-time routines of Slovene girls, and once grown, most Slovene women work out regularly. In the warm weather, you can see small groups of women practicing their gymnastic skills in the parks and on the beaches of Slovenia.

Women are also increasingly taking up chess. Traditionally a game for men, it has always been taken seriously in Slovenia. Laura Unuk is the country's top female player. She achieved the title of Woman International Grandmaster in 2019.

Some other great female Slovene athletes include the downhill skier Tina Maze, who won two gold medals at the 2014 Winter Olympics. She retired in 2017 after a spectacular career. Petra Majdic, a cross-country skiing champion, was once called the best female athlete in Slovenia. Urska Zolnir is a retired judo champ. In 2012, she became the first Slovene woman to win an Olympic gold medal.

INTERNET LINKS

https://www.climbing.com/places/climb-slovenia-the-thousand-faces-of-central-europes-karstic-gem
This article provides a first-person account of mountain climbing adventures in Slovenia.

https://nba.nbcsports.com/2019/11/03/lebron-james-says-luka-doncic-just-plays-the-game-the-right-way
This article poses the question: Is Luka Doncic the new LeBron James?

https://www.total-slovenia-news.com/lifestyle/487-laura-unuk-18-year-old-slovenian-chess-sensation
Chess champion Laura Unuk is the subject of this article.

FESTIVALS

A green fairy with a chameleon brings joy and excitement to children waiting for the Grandfather Frost Parade in Ljubljana on December 27, 2012.

12

BEING A PREDOMINANTLY CHRISTIAN nation, Slovenia follows the church calendar in its holiday celebrations. The year brings the religious highlights of Easter and Christmas, along with spring's Whit Sunday (Pentecost) and the Assumption of Mary on August 15. Oddly, perhaps, for a Catholic nation, the country also celebrates Reformation Day on October 31. This official holiday marks the Protestant Reformation in the 16th century. The following day, November 1, brings Remembrance Day, or All Saints' Day. This is a day to visit cemeteries and honor dead relatives.

Alongside the religious holidays, Slovenes celebrate secular and national holidays as well. Patriotic holidays include the Day of Uprising Against Occupation, or Resistance Day, on April 27, which commemorates fighting against Nazi occupiers in World War II; Statehood Day on June 25, which marks the country's declaration of independence from Yugoslavia in 1991; and Independence and Unity Day on December 26, which both extends the Christmas holiday and remembers the official proclamation of the Slovene independence referendum in 1990.

Preseren Day, February 8, is a public holiday in honor of the Slovene national poet France Preseren, who died on that date in 1849. The holiday also celebrates Slovene culture in general and is a day off from work or school for most people. Many museums open their doors for free that day, and the poet's hometown throws a party.

Those are far from the only festivities in a Slovene year. Summer is the height of festival season, marked by many traditional and colorful celebrations. The symbol of Slovene festivals is a springtime figure born of pagan legend who works his supernatural powers to chase winter away. His name is Kurent, and today he is both a national symbol and a mythic presence at all Slovene festivals.

THE BELLS OF KURENT

The legend of Kurent originated in Slovenia's oldest city of Ptuj, where the main Kurentovanje festival is celebrated each year. However, Kurent is a major figure at Carnival festivities throughout the country. The revels take place on Shrove Tuesday in February, the day before Ash Wednesday, the first day of Lent. (Lent is the 40-day season of somber anticipation of Christ's death and resurrection.) On that Tuesday, children and adults wearing traditional Kurent masks and costumes run through the streets. Kurent wears long-haired

Large and small Kurent characters parade on the streets of Ormoz during Carnival 2019.

sheepskins adorned with cowbells. He often carries a club. Kurents (or Kurenti) run skipping and jumping so that their bells ring loudly enough to scare the cold winter away. Young girls in colorful peasant dresses offer handkerchiefs to those masquerading as Kurent. Housewives break clay pots at their feet for good luck and offer an age-old incantation: "Who tells a tale always adds a word." With this truth they acknowledge that the legend of Kurent grows from added word to added word.

While Shrove Tuesday is the high point of the homage to Kurent, festivities take place during the days both before and after it. Revelers parade through the streets wearing a variety of masks called *laufarji*. These can be modeled after creatures out of Slovene mythology, or they can be caricatures of modern politicians. The main parades feature colorful floats and marching bands or strolling fiddlers. Carnivals vary from place to place. One of the most colorful is in Cerknica, where local tradition calls for a variety of witches' costumes.

Food plays a large part in the Kurent festivals. The start of the festivities used to be marked by cooking a pig's head, but today the kickoff meal is more likely to be smoked ham. Fried doughnuts are traditional, and children go from door to door soliciting doughnuts, other goodies, or small sums of money. A very old ritual consists of giving wood logs to unmarried people, who then must donate money toward a sort of singles party. On Ash Wednesday, the day after Shrove Tuesday, a stuffed figure of Kurent is buried in a ceremony to mark the end of winter. Finally, the feasting concludes with the serving of the *potica* (po-TEE-tza), the traditional Slovene dessert cake.

MUSIC FESTIVALS

Music fills the valleys and bounces off the mountainsides of Slovenia during the months of July and August. Festivals of every musical genre compete with one another all summer long. Every city and village has a program to offer, and impromptu street performances are common.

The most popular cultural celebrations are annual summer festivals featuring not only music but theater and dance performances as well. These are held in both Ljubljana and Bled between the end of June and the beginning

CHRISTMAS IN SLOVENIA

At Christmastime, Slovenia lights up like a fairy tale. Elaborate displays of Christmas lights and bedecked fir trees illuminate city streets and small town centers.

Traditional Western celebrations of Christmas are relatively new to Slovenia. Prior to the country's independence in 1991, those traditions were not well known. Communist Yugoslavia followed Soviet tradition in downplaying (or banning) religion and replacing religious traditions with new, state-sanctioned

The old city center in Ljubljana is aglow with Christmas lights and decorations.

holidays. In that way, the great gift-giving holiday became New Year's Day during the communist era, and the Russian "Grandfather Frost"—Ded Moroz, or Dedek Mraz in Slovene—replaced Saint Nicholas as the legendary figure of the winter season. Today, however, Slovenia is free to embrace all the Santa figures: Saint Nicholas, also known as Father Christmas; the American Santa Claus, who is becoming more mainstream as American popular culture spreads across the world; and Grandfather Frost.

As in much of Europe, Saint Nicholas, called Miklavz in Slovenia, arrives on his feast day, December 6. This Old World Father Christmas harkens back to the real Saint Nicholas (ca. 270–342 CE), an early Christian bishop from a village in today's Turkey. His generosity to those in need and his love for children developed after his death into the legend of Saint Nicholas. This white-bearded figure dresses in the long robe and miter hat of a bishop. On the eve of his feast day, he leaves small gifts in children's shoes or stockings. These include candy, fruit, or little toys.

In Slovenia, the jolly Santa of North Pole fame is called Bozicek. For Slovenes who have embraced the myth, Bozicek leaves his gifts on the eve of Christ's birth—Christmas Eve.

The third gift-bringer arrives on New Year's Eve. Like Santa, he is decked in furs and wears a long white beard. However, Grandfather Frost wears white or blue and rides through Slovenia in a carriage pulled by two white horses.

At Christmas markets and festivities throughout Slovenia, any or all of these magical folk are likely to be seen, bringing joy to children and reminding them to be good.

of September. During the same period, Brezice, in the hills of the Posavje region, offers its annual early music festival. This world-renowned event features music ranging from the medieval to Beethoven, performed on the authentic instruments of the relevant periods. From its beginning in 1983, under the artistic direction of Klemen Ramovs, it has attracted top international performers. Many of the Brezice concerts take place in the acoustically outstanding Knight's Hall, the high-ceilinged chamber of a Renaissance castle. Other performances are held in the Mokrice Castle, with its impressively decorated floors, and in the huge arcaded courtyard of the Kostanjevica Monastery.

The Kostanjevica Monastery is also known for its yearly summer series of concerts called Music from the Gardens of Saint Frances. The concerts typically feature Slovene musicians from the surrounding area, as well as

The courtyard of the Kostanjevica Monastery is often the venue for music performances.

musicians from Italy. Selections vary from those of the baroque era to the works of 19th-century romantic composers.

TRNOVFEST

A more varied, and more modern, event is the Trnovfest (formerly Trnfest) series held every August in Ljubljana's Trnovo district. The lively, month-long program celebrates alternative arts and culture. It's usually packed with enthusiastic beer drinkers, making it a shoulder-to-shoulder experience of Slovene socializing. The crowd is usually good-natured, and incidents of violence are rare.

In addition to the concerts, Trnovfest may offer workshops in African dance, acting techniques, batik painting on clothing, and other disciplines. There are also creative workshops for children. Some evenings, there are parties with professional or amateur DJs.

JAZZ, PUPPETS, AND COWS

The Ljubljana Jazz Festival is Europe's oldest continually running jazz festival. In 2019, it celebrated 60 years of celebrating the musical genre that was born in the African American culture of the United States, but which now envelopes the world.

The International Saxophone Meeting and Competition in Nova Gorica celebrates an instrument that is native to the world of jazz. Saxophone players from all over the world flock to the Nova Gorica Cultural Center to play their instruments during this unique jam session. The music tends to be mostly blues and traditional jazz.

Not just music but folklore, crafts, and local culture highlight the Lent Festival held from late June to early July in Slovenia's second-largest city, Maribor. Summertime is also when the Maribor Puppet Theater hosts the International Puppet Festival, which attracts puppeteers from all over the world. Each year, children of all ages and all language groups are entertained by new puppet plays.

In mid-September, the mooing of the cows descending to the valleys from their high pasturelands heralds the Kravji Bal (Cows' Ball) festival in the Bohinj Valley. Platters of steaming food draw crowds. Once people have eaten and drunk their fill, the country-style folk dancing begins. As couples slip in and out of the various reels, the dancing continues nonstop until the weekend-long Cows' Ball is over.

The Kravji Ball celebrates the return of cattle from the high pastures where they graze in summer.

MOVIES AND DRESSAGE

Slovenia hosts a variety of fall and winter festivals. In October, the International Festival of Contemporary Arts—City of Women, a festival in Ljubljana of contemporary female artists, presents the works of women painters, sculptors, and performance artists, plus a variety of other artistic endeavors produced by women.

The Ljubljana International Film Festival is held in November. The aim of the festival is to introduce Slovene audiences and visiting film buffs to the best movies—regardless of where they were produced, what the size of the budget was, or the stardom status of the cast. During the selection process, special attention is paid to the work of new and as yet unrecognized directors. In December, Slovenia's Festival of Gay and Lesbian Film (FGLF) is presented. Begun in 1984, the FGLF is the oldest such festival in Europe.

Winter sports events begin in January with various kinds of skiing competitions and dog sled races. These attract hardy athletes to the beautiful mountainous regions of the country.

In May, dressage competitions are held in Lipica, near the Italian border. Dressage is an exhibition of horsemanship in which the horse is put through a series of difficult movements by the very slight movements of its rider. It is an art form as precise as a ballet and requires months of training for both horse

The canines of an enthusiastic dog sled team go for the glory at a competition in Kranjska Gora.

and rider. The most famous horses in dressage competitions are the all-white Lipizzaners, once the steeds of Austrian royalty and of the Emperor's Royal Guard. For hundreds of years, horses bred in Lipica have been considered the *créme de la créme* of the Lipizzaner breed. International dressage competitions offer a rare opportunity to see these magnificent prancing white steeds of Slovenia at their very best.

INTERNET LINKS

http://www.kurentovanje.net/en/main
This is the site of the Kurentovanje festival in Ptuj.

https://www.slovenia.info/en
A myriad of special events are listed on this official Slovenia tourism site.

https://theculturetrip.com/europe/slovenia/articles/the-best-festivals-in-slovenia
This travel site lists some of the more unusual festivals in Slovenia.

https://www.timeanddate.com/holidays/slovenia/2021
This calendar site presents the holidays and observances in Slovenia.

FOOD

A woman sells local vegetables at the market in Maribor.

13

SLOVENE CUISINE IS BASED ON

hearty cooking and inexpensive ingredients. It's influenced by the cooking styles of the region, with aspects of Austrian, Hungarian, German, Czech, Italian, and Balkan cooking. The result is a collection of delicious culinary offerings.

TRADITIONAL DISHES

Slovenes tend to be active and athletic, and it follows that they are hearty eaters. Their traditional dishes reflect long days spent plowing the fields of Pomurje, digging the coal of Zasavje, laboring in the ironworks of Koroska, or skiing the icy slopes of the Julian Alps in Gorenjska.

Typical Slovene dishes feature meat, carbohydrates (potatoes, rice, corn, pasta, or wheat), and vegetables. Roasts or stews are the usual meal for the ordinary Slovene three times a week or more. Roasted meats and cutlets are mostly made of pork or veal. Braised venison and slow-cooked chicken-in-a-pot are also popular, as is the Slovene version of meatloaf, which contains raisins. Beef or veal goulash, called *golaz* (GO-lash), is sometimes prepared Hungarian-style with paprika on a bed of broad noodles.

Staples for other days, particularly for poorer people, are *zganci* (DZGAN-tzi), a peasant dish made of buckwheat or maize porridge and served with sauerkraut, and *zlikrofi* (DZLEE-kro-fee), a sort of ravioli filled with potato, onion, and bacon. *Ricet* (REE-chet) is a barley porridge with vegetables and sausage.

Festive occasions, especially Christmas, New Year's, and Easter, call for *potica*. The rolled cake or sweet bread can be made with an astonishing variety of fillings, but walnut, hazelnut, poppy seed, cottage cheese, and even tarragon are among the most popular. The pastry is baked in a log shape or ring, and the slices show off a pretty spiral of filling.

Traditional Slovene *zlikrofi*, or potato dumplings, are served with a bacon and mushroom sauce.

As well as being prepared at home, these are the dishes most often served in Slovene restaurants or inns. However, just as in most US cities, Slovene cities boast a wide variety of ethnic restaurants and foods. Italian restaurants, most common in the cities close to the Italian border, offer pizza, a variety of pasta, and fish, mussels, and calamari (squid) prepared in Venetian-style stews. Fish broiled with olive oil, olives, garlic, and tomatoes reflects a Greek influence. There are also Thai, Indonesian, and Mexican restaurants offering specialties that are sometimes prepared with a uniquely Slovene twist to the usual recipe.

SOUPS

Most meals start out with soup, particularly in fall and winter. Slovene soups tend to be hearty and thick. Some of them border on being stews. A goulash soup containing meat, carrots, and dumplings, and seasoned with hot paprika, is distinguished from the goulash main dish only by the size of the portion. Fresh mushroom soup is a favorite in Slovene homes and is on the menu in most restaurants, where it is usually garnished with a dollop of whipped cream. Mushrooms are also to be found in other Slovene soups. A rich, savory garlic soup is a favorite for Slovenes who like to dunk their crusty bread. Vegetable soup is served with chunks of fresh vegetables, both cooked and raw. Tomato soup, made with heavy cream, is extra thick. A variety of fish soups may be found in the eateries of towns and cities of Slovenia's coastal area. Sauerkraut soup is a winter staple in the colder rural areas, and a variety of herb cream soups welcome skiers back from a day on the Julian Alps.

BLACK KITCHENS

Throughout Slovenia, both in the Karavanke Mountains of the Savinjsko region and in the rural farm areas, home cooking, particularly baking, is done in the crna kuhinja (*CERN-a KOO-hin-ya*), or *"black kitchen." It is likely that the name comes from the fact that black kitchens traditionally had an open fireplace and no chimney, an arrangement resulting in a sooty film settling on the walls and counters. Possibly because of smoke, some black kitchens—but not all—are separate structures from the homes of the families for whom the food is being prepared.*

In farm families, it is traditionally the women who do the cooking while the men labor long hours in the fields. However, in cities, and even in many villages, as women claim their place in Slovene society, more and more men are sharing the cooking and cleaning chores. Many younger Slovene men take great pride in their innovative recipes.

Black kitchens, though, are still mainly the domain of rural women. Most feature old-fashioned wood-burning tile stoves. The firebox inside the stove is lined with refractory bricks—bricks that can withstand very high temperatures. The upper body of the stove interior is made of ordinary bricks. The tiles on the outside of the stove hold in the heat and remain relatively cool to the touch. Some tile stoves are centuries old and are considered antiques. Stovecraft, the production of tiles for stoves, flourished as an art form in Slovenia and other Central European countries between 1870 and the late 1920s. Some of this work is still to be found in Slovene black kitchens today.

BREAD, CAKES, AND PIES

The fame of black kitchens and wood-burning tile stoves was spread by the palate-pleasing breads, cakes, and pies produced in them. Bread is both a staple and a delicacy for Slovenes. Bread and rolls made in tile stoves are preferred for their texture and tastiness. Peasant breads, as they are known, tend to be crusted, grainy, and chewy. These breads come in many varieties, including whole wheat, rye, sourdough, and—a favorite in the Savinjsko region—traditional white-flour bread with a hard crust and a softer, almost fluffy, center. Slovene specialties include applesauce bread, grilled cinnamon bread, and shredded-wheat bread. An alternative to bread is savory muffins made of corn, wheat, or rice (often spread carefully with soft, farm-fresh butter or jam).

Black kitchens also cater to the Slovene sweet tooth. Among the uniquely Slovene baked goods are Jule cake bursting with almonds and cherries, beautifully browned doughnuts made with nutmeg and sprinkled with sugar, sour cream twists, apple kuchen, apricot turnovers, Christmas

This typical potica, baked in a ring mold, has a walnut filling.

plum pudding, and *kolachki* (ko-LATCH-kee), or cookies filled with apricot jam or walnut paste.

Flacanti (FLAN-tza-ti) are traditional Slovene cookies made with cinnamon, poppy seeds, or various jams. Potica, with its variety of succulent ingredients rolled in a tender dough, is considered the Slovene national cake. Pies of every kind—Bavarian chocolate, meringue, sweet potato, and all sorts of fruit in many styles of pie crusts—may be sampled in the different regions of Slovenia. Wild bilberry pie, made from a fruit native to the Balkans, offers a sweet-and-sour taste.

PICNICS

At the first hint of warmer weather in the non-alpine areas of the country, Slovene families pack a picnic basket and head for the woods, the fields, or the banks of rivers. They may set up an outdoor barbecue or build an outdoor fire and toast or grill hot dogs or klobasa, which are large sausages that differ in

Klobasa, a pork sausage, is traditionally served with cooked, shredded cabbage.

A cheese burek is a savory treat with parsley, cream, onion, and garlic.

their spiciness from region to region. If it's too hot to barbecue, picnickers will bring along sandwiches of local cheese and salami. Cheeses may vary greatly in consistency and taste from village to village. Sandwiches are usually made from fresh-baked bread, prepared either at home or in the brick ovens of a local bakery.

In addition to sandwiches, quick lunches for hikers include the popular Slovene snack bars, which come in a variety ranging from what some might term junk food to traditional and vegan health foods. Fresh fruit and raw vegetables are also popular trail foods.

For the uphill climber, a *burek* (BOO-rek), a flaky pastry filled with cheese, might be purchased from one of the many street kiosks found in both metropolitan areas and larger villages. These pastries can provide that needed burst of energy to reach the top of a hill.

BILBERRIES, DANDELIONS, AND MUSHROOMS

Carrying pails, buckets, jars, and baskets of all sizes, Slovene adults and children of all ages take to the heaths and woods from July to September, when wild bilberry bushes produce their fruit. The shrubs are short and squat with wiry branches and globular leaves with a waxy surface. The berries are a blackish-blue color and delicious when freshly picked. Although they are from the same family as blueberries, bilberries have a more pronounced flavor. They are often made into jams and jellies and preserved in large quantities to last through the autumn and winter. They can also be made into cookies or used as a filling for pies. Slovenes enjoy a bilberry tea, and bilberry extract is both used as a dietary supplement and sold in health-food stores for its medicinal qualities. These include preventing night blindness, strengthening eyesight, and counteracting diarrhea.

Before the bilberry-picking season opens, beginning in early spring, the hillsides in southern and central Slovenia welcome hundreds of people

Picking wild bilberries is a seasonal endeavor.

looking for wild dandelions—or, to be more accurate, dandelion shoots. Bending over to peer at the sloped ground, these sharp-eyed pickers select only the very young plants, discarding the ones whose flowers are fully formed because their shoots will be bitter. There are several kinds of edible dandelions, and none are poisonous, but the ones with serrated leaves and whitish stems are the tastiest. These are used to make traditional Slovene dandelion salad, a hearty dish prepared with peeled and sliced potatoes, hard-boiled eggs, chopped garlic, wine vinegar, lard with cracklings, and salt. A more modern version leaves out the lard and adds healthier vegetable oils.

A spring salad features young dandelion leaves with parmesan cheese, cracklings, eggs, chicory, and lettuce.

The practice of foraging for wild mushrooms in Slovenia is so popular that it has been called a national sport. More than 70 varieties of edible mushrooms grow in the forests. Some of these have been so heavily picked that certain species are in danger of becoming extinct. To prevent this, legislation has been passed limiting how many can be plucked over a 24-hour period. Meaty, tasty mushrooms, low in calories and containing no fat, find their way into a wide variety of Slovene dishes. They are eaten raw, as snacks; are ever present as garnishes for fowl, venison, and other meats; add flavor and body to a variety of stews; and are used as filling in a popular pastry sold by street vendors. Although mushrooms are a fungus and not a vegetable, many Slovenes regard them as the tastiest vegetable of all.

BEVERAGES

Wines are drunk moderately with most dinner and lunch meals by many Slovenes. The regions of Podravje, Posavje, and Pomurje produce most of the wines in the country. Beer halls in the cities of Slovenia serve a native *pivo* (PEE-vo), or beer, under the brand name Lasko Zlatorog, which is quite popular.

Liquors include plum brandy, pear brandy, and brandies made from other fruits.

Kava (KA-va), or coffee, heads the list of nonalcoholic drinks that Slovenes prefer. In the home, it's consumed black, or with sugar and milk or cream. In midafternoon, espresso and cappuccino are preferred over ordinary coffee in the small café bars. *Caj* (CHAI), or tea, is usually served black, and tea variations such as pink tea and tea punch are popular. Also popular is a Slovene punch made out of four kinds of fruit juice, crushed pineapple, and almond flavoring. Mineral water and carbonated beverages are also available. These are usually consumed with midafternoon pastry snacks or small, crustless sandwiches.

People enjoy the sun and a good bite to eat at a street café in the Old Town section of Ljubljana.

INTERNET LINKS

https://greenhills.si/traditional-slovenian-food
The country's "Top 10" traditional foods are pictured and described.

https://www.travlinmad.com/blog/traditional-slovenian-food -guide
This site provides a comprehensive guide to regional food specialties in Slovenia.

RICET (SLOVENE BARLEY PORRIDGE)

This dish can be a porridge, stew, or soup depending on the amount of liquid added.

2 tablespoons vegetable oil
3 carrots, sliced
2 stalks celery, chopped
1 leek, cleaned and sliced
1 onion, chopped
3 cloves garlic, minced
2 tomatoes, chopped, or small can
   diced tomatoes
1 cup (200 grams) pearl barley
6—8 cups (1.4—1.9 liters) water
   or stock
2 bay leaves
¾ pound (350 g) smoked sausage, cut into bite-sized pieces
1 15-ounce (425 g) can pinto or white beans
Fresh parsley or dill, chopped
Salt and pepper to taste

Sauté the carrots, celery, leek, and onion in oil over medium heat until soft. Add garlic and cook for another few seconds.

Add tomatoes, barley, water or stock, bay leaves, and salt and pepper.

Bring to a boil, cover, and simmer about 30 minutes or until barley is tender.

Stir in the sausage and beans and cook another 5 to 10 minutes.

Stir in parsley or dill and adjust seasonings to taste.

LAKE BLED CREAM CAKE

2 puff pastry sheets (store bought; thawed according to directions on package)
4 cups (1 liter) whole milk
8 eggs, separated into yolks and whites
1 cup (200 grams) sugar
1 ¼ cups (180 g) flour
2 teaspoons vanilla extract
3 cups (710 milliliters) heavy whipping cream
2 tablespoons powdered (confectioners) sugar, plus more
    for sprinkling

Preheat the oven to 350°F (175°C).

Pastry: On a lightly floured work surface, roll each sheet of puff pastry into a 9x13-inch rectangle. Place the pastry on a baking sheet and bake for 10 minutes.

Remove the pastry from the oven and set aside to cool completely.

Custard: In large bowl, beat egg yolks with sugar until light and fluffy. Slowly add in flour, vanilla extract, and 1 cup of milk until well combined. Set aside.

Over medium heat, boil remaining 3 cups of milk in a sauce pan. Slowly stir in egg yolk mixture and keep stirring until thickened. Remove from heat and set aside.

In a large bowl, beat the 8 egg whites until very stiff. Fold into the custard.

Assemble: Place one pastry sheet on the bottom of a 9x13-inch (23x33 cm) baking dish. Pour the custard over the pastry. Place plastic wrap over custard and chill in the refrigerator for a few hours until cooled and firm.

Beat the heavy whipping cream with the powdered sugar until firm peaks form. Pour over the chilled custard and smooth. Cut the second pastry sheet into 15 squares. Place over the custard cake in neat rows and sprinkle with more powdered sugar.

Serve cold by cutting between the pastry squares.

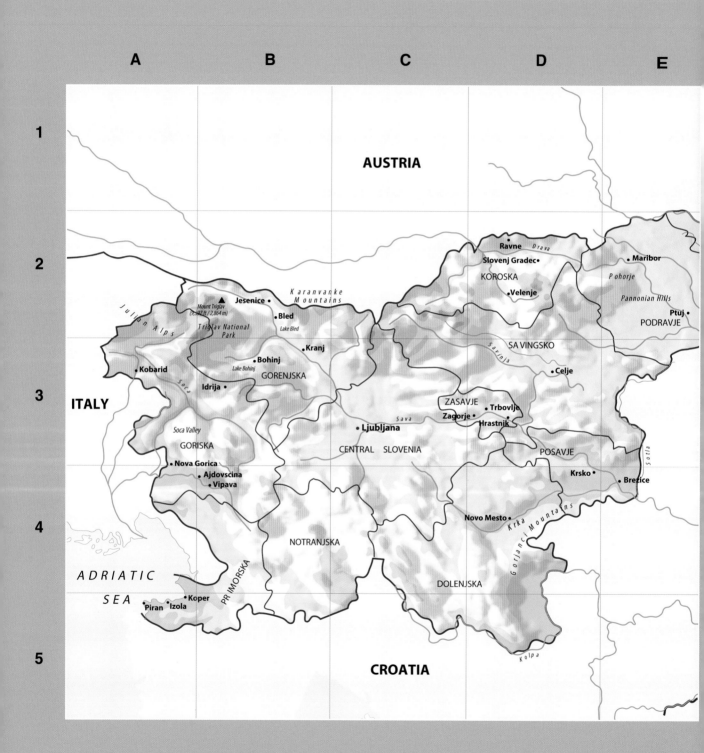

MAP OF SLOVENIA

F

HUNGARY

• Murska Sobota

• Slovenske Gorice

POMURJE

Capital city
Major town
Mountain park

Feet	Meters
9,900	3,000
6,600	2,000
3,300	1,000
1,650	500
660	200
0	0

Adriatic Sea,
  A4—A5
Ajdovscina, B4
Austria, A2—F1

Bled, B2
Bohinj, B3
Brezice, E4

Celje, D3
Central Slovenia,
  B3—D3
Croatia, A5—F2

Dolenjska, C4—D5
Drava (river),
  A1—F3

Gorenjska, A2—C3
Goriska, A2—B4
Gorjanci
  Mountains,
  D4—E4

Hrastnik, D3
Hungary, F1—F2

Idrija, B3
Italy, A2—B4
Izola, A5

Jesenice, B2
Julian Alps, A2—B2

Karavanke
  Mountains,
  B2—C2
Kobarid, A3
Kolpa (river),
  C4—D5
Koper, A5
Koroska, C2—D2
Kranj, B3
Krsko, D4

Lake Bled, B2
Lake Bohinj, B3
Ljubljana, C3

Maribor, E2
Mount Triglav, B2
Mura (river),
  D1—F2
Murska Sobota, F2

Notranjska, B4—
  C5
Nova Gorica, A3
Novo Mesto, D4

Pannonian hills, E2
Piran, A5
Podravje, D2—F2
Pohorje Mountains,
  E2
Pomurje, E2—F2

Posavje, D3—E4
Primorska, A4—B5
Ptuj, E2

Ravne, D2

Sava (river), B3—F5
Savinja (river),
  C2—D3
Savinjsko, C2—E3
Slovenj Gradec, D2
Slovenske Gorice,
  F2
Soca (river),
  A3—A4
Sotla (river),
  E3—E4

Trbovlje, D3
Triglav National
  Park, A2—B3

Velenje, D2
Vipava, B4

Zagorje, D3
Zasavje, C3—D3

ECONOMIC SLOVENIA

Agriculture	Natural Resources	Services
Corn	Al Aluminum	Airport
Dairy Products	Coal	
Wheat	Hydroelectricity	**Manufacturing**
Wine	Lead	Ferrous metallurgy
	Mercury	
	Nuclear reactor	
	Zinc	

ABOUT THE ECONOMY

All figures are 2017 estimates unless otherwise noted.

GROSS DOMESTIC PRODUCT (OFFICIAL EXCHANGE RATE)
$48.87 billion

GDP BY SECTOR OF ORIGIN
Agriculture: 1.8 percent
Industry: 32.2 percent
Services: 65.9 percent

INFLATION RATE
1.4 percent

CURRENCY
Euro (EUR) €
$1 USD = 0.90 euro (2019)

AGRICULTURAL PRODUCTS
hops, wheat, coffee, corn, apples, pears, cattle, sheep, poultry

NATURAL RESOURCES
lignite, lead, zinc, building stone, hydropower, forests

MAJOR EXPORTS
manufactured goods, machinery and transportation equipment, chemicals, food

MAJOR IMPORTS
machinery and transportation equipment, manufactured goods, chemicals, fuels and lubricants, food

MAIN TRADING PARTNERS
Germany, Italy, Croatia, Austria, Turkey, France, China

WORKFORCE
959,000

LABOR FORCE BY OCCUPATION
Agriculture: 5.5 percent
Industry: 31.2 percent
Services: 63.3 percent

UNEMPLOYMENT RATE
6.6 percent

POPULATION BELOW POVERTY LINE
13.9 percent (2016)

CULTURAL SLOVENIA

Soca Valley
During World War I, Austrian and Italian troops fought many bloody battles near the borders of Austria and Italy in this part of Slovenia.

The Julian Alps, Mount Triglav
Located in the Julian Alps in the Gorenjska Region, Mount Triglav is the highest peak and a national symbol of Slovenia.

Bled Castle
This exquisite example of a medieval castle is located at the top of Lake Bled.

The Bell of Wishes
On the western end of the island in Lake Bled is a 15th-century belfry. There is an old tradition that anyone who rings the bell will get what they wish for.

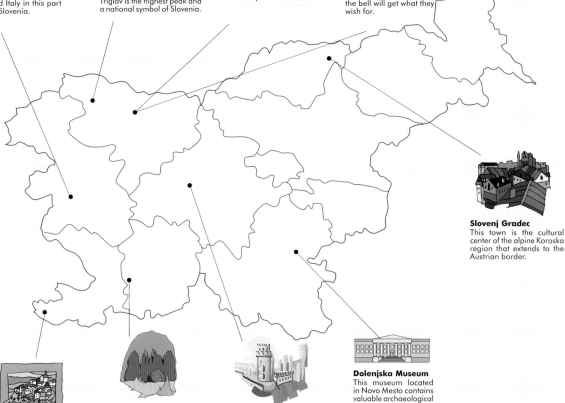

Slovenj Gradec
This town is the cultural center of the alpine Koroska region that extends to the Austrian border.

Dolenjska Museum
This museum located in Novo Mesto contains valuable archaeological finds, as well as more modern collections.

Piran
A beach town on the Adriatic Coast, picturesque Piran is a treasure trove of Venetian gothic architecture and narrow streets.

The Skocjan Caves
In the karst region in southwestern Slovenia, this labyrinth of caves and springs includes an enormous canyon, underground caverns, and rivers.

Ljubljana Castle
Dating from the 11th century, this castle on a hill above the historic section of Ljubljana has served as a royal residence and a prison.

All figures are 2018 estimates unless otherwise noted.

OFFICIAL NAME
Republika Slovenija (Republic of Slovenia)

CAPITAL
Ljubljana

DESCRIPTION OF FLAG
It has three equal horizontal bands of white (top), blue, and red, with the Slovene seal (a shield with the image of Triglav, Slovenia's highest peak, in white). Beneath the peak are two wavy blue lines depicting seas and rivers, and above it are three six-pointed stars arranged in an inverted triangle, taken from the coat of arms of the Counts of Celje, the great Slovene dynastic house of the late 14th and early 15th centuries. The seal is in the upper hoist side of the flag, centered in the white and blue bands.

LAND AREA
7,825 square miles (20,273 sq km)

POPULATION
2,102,126

POPULATION GROWTH RATE
0.03 percent

BIRTH RATE
9.2 births per 1,000 people

ETHNIC GROUPS
Slovene 83.1 percent, Serb 2 percent, Croat 1.8 percent, Bosnian 1.1 percent, other or unspecified 12 percent (2002 census)

RELIGIONS
Catholic 57.8 percent, Muslim 2.4 percent, Orthodox 2.3 percent, other Christian 0.9 percent, unaffiliated 3.5 percent, other or unspecified 23 percent, none 10.1 percent (2002 census)

LANGUAGES
Slovene (official) 91.1 percent, Serbo-Croatian 4.5 percent, other or unspecified 4.4 percent, Italian (official, only in municipalities where Italian national communities reside), Hungarian (official, only in municipalities where Hungarian national communities reside) (2002 census)

LIFE EXPECTANCY AT BIRTH
Total population: 81.2 years
Male: 78.3 years
Female: 84.2 years

LITERACY RATE
99.7 percent (2015)

TIMELINE

IN SLOVENIA	IN THE WORLD
	753 BCE
300s BCE	Rome is founded.
The future Slovenia, Croatia, and Bosnia-Herzegovina become part of the Roman Empire.	
500s CE	
Ancestors of Slovenes settle in the Julian Alps.	**600 CE**
623	The Maya civilization reaches its height.
King Samo establishes the Slovene kingdom.	**1054**
1144	The Great Schism divides the Catholic
First records mention Ljubljana by name.	Church into Eastern and Western churches—
1300s	Orthodox Catholic and Roman Catholic.
The Hapsburg Empire rules Slovenia until 1918.	**1530**
1550	The transatlantic slave trade begins.
The first book in Slovene is printed.	**1558–1603**
	Elizabeth I rules England.
	1776
	The US Declaration of Independence is signed.
	1789–1799
	The French Revolution takes place.
1838	
The first railway, part of the Vienna–Trieste route, is built in Slovenia.	**1861**
	The US Civil War begins.
1869	**1869**
Thirty thousand people at Vizmarje demand a united Slovenia.	The Suez Canal opens.
	1914
1918	World War I begins.
The Kingdom of Serbs, Croats, and Slovenes is created.	
1929	
King Alexander I renames the country the Kingdom of Yugoslavia.	**1939**
1944	World War II begins.
Tito becomes prime minister of Yugoslavia.	
1945	**1945**
Slovenia becomes a state of communist Yugoslavia.	World War II ends with the US bombing of Japan.
	1949
	The North Atlantic Treaty Organization (NATO) is formed.

IN SLOVENIA	IN THE WORLD
	1966–1969 The Chinese Cultural Revolution occurs. **1969** US astronaut Neil Armstrong walks on the moon.
1980 Tito dies in Ljubljana.	**1986** Nuclear power disaster affects Chernobyl in Ukraine.
1991 Slovenia declares its independence from Yugoslavia.	**1991** The Soviet Union collapses.
1992 Slovenia joins the United Nations.	**1997** Hong Kong is returned to China. **2001** Terrorists attack the United States on 9/11. **2003** The Iraq War begins.
2004 Slovenia joins the European Union. **2007** Slovenia adopts the European currency, the euro. **2008** Borut Pahor becomes prime minister.	**2008** The United States elects its first African American president, Barack Obama. **2009** An outbreak of H1N1 flu spreads around the world.
2012 Janez Jansa become prime minister. Thousands protest anti-austerity measures in Ljubljana, and Maribor. Borut Pahor wins presidential run-off.	
2015 Voters in a referendum reject legislation that would have granted same-sex couples the right to marry.	**2015–2016** ISIS launches terror attacks in Belgium and France. **2017** Donald Trump becomes US president. Hurricanes devastate Houston, Texas; Puerto Rico; and other Caribbean islands.
2018 Marjan Sarec becomes prime minister.	**2018** The Winter Olympics are held in South Korea.
2019 Postal workers go on strike in November, demanding a pay raise and an increase in staff.	**2019** Notre Dame Cathedral in Paris is damaged by fire. US President Trump is impeached.

GLOSSARY

black kitchens, or *crna kuhinja* (CERN-a KOO-hin-ya)
Kitchens with an open fireplace and no chimney where, in rural areas, traditional baking is still done.

despot
One who exercises power tyrannically.

Drzavni Zbor
The National Assembly; the legislative branch of the Slovene government.

European Union (EU)
An organization of European countries dedicated to increasing economic integration and strengthening cooperation among its members.

Germanization
The spread of German words and expressions that have become a part of everyday Slovene language.

Hapsburgs
The German royal family who ruled Austria from 1278 to 1918.

karst
A limestone area of underground caves, caverns, and rivers.

Kurent
A Carnival spirit; an early springtime figure born of pagan legend who allegedly worked his supernatural powers to chase winter away.

***klobasa* (klo-BA-sa)**
A type of sausage.

laufarji
Masks that portray creatures in Slovene myth, worn on Shrove Tuesday.

Lipizzaners
All-white performing horses of the royal Austrian court of the Hapsburgs, still performing today.

NATO
The North Atlantic Treaty Organization. An intergovernmental military alliance between North American and European countries.

Natura 2000
A network of protected areas throughout the European Union countries.

***potica* (po-TEE-za)**
The Slovene national cake.

FOR FURTHER INFORMATION

BOOKS

Blake, Jason. *Slovenia—Culture Smart! The Essential Guide to Customs and Culture*. London, UK: Kuperand, 2011.

DK Eyewitness. *Slovenia*. New York, NY: DK Penguin Random House, 2017.

Lonely Planet, Mark Baker, Anthony Ham, and Jessica Lee. *Slovenia*. Melbourne, Australia: Lonely Planet, 2019.

Luthar, Oto. *The Land Between: A History of Slovenia*. Bern, Switzerland: Peter Lang Publishing, 2013.

ONLINE

BBC News Slovenia Country Profile. https://www.bbc.com/news/world-europe-17846376.

CIA. *The World Factbook*. "Slovenia." https://www.cia.gov/library/publications/the-world-factbook/geos/si.html.

Encyclopedia Britannica. "Slovenia." https://www.britannica.com/place/Slovenia.

I Feel Slovenia. https://www.slovenia.info/en.

Lonely Planet. "Slovenia." https://www.lonelyplanet.com/slovenia.

Republic of Slovenia. https://www.gov.si/en.

Slovenia Times. http://www.sloveniatimes.com.

Total Slovenia News. https://www.total-slovenia-news.com.

FILMS AND VIDEOS

Oda Preserenu ("Ode to the Poet"). Slovene with English subtitles. Directed by Martin Srebotnjak, 2001.

Rick Steves' Europe: Bulgaria, Eastern Turkey, Slovenia, and Croatia. Back Door Productions, 2000.

The Seasoned Traveler: Slovenia. Createspace, 2005.

BIBLIOGRAPHY

BBC News Slovenia Country Profile. https://www.bbc.com/news/world-europe-17846376.

CIA. *The World Factbook*. "Slovenia." https://www.cia.gov/library/publications/the-world-factbook/geos/si.html.

Diedrich, Cajus G. "'Neanderthal Bone Flutes': Simply Products of Ice Age Spotted Hyena Scavenging Activities on Cave Bear Cubs in European Cave Bear Dens." *Royal Society*, April 1, 2015. https://royalsocietypublishing.org/doi/full/10.1098/rsos.140022.

Encyclopedia Britannica. "Slovenia." https://www.britannica.com/place/Slovenia.

Export.gov. "Slovenia—Agricultural Sector." February 19, 2019. https://www.export.gov/article?id=SloveniaAgriculturalSector.

Josipovic, Damir. "Slovenia and the Census: From the 20th Century Yugoslav Counts to the Register-Based Census of 2011." *Contemporary Southeastern Europe*, 2015. http://www.contemporarysee.org/sites/default/files/papers/josipovic_slo_census.pdf.

Institute for Economics and Peace. "Global Peace Index 2019." http://visionofhumanity.org/indexes/global-peace-index.

Lonely Planet. "Slovenia." https://www.lonelyplanet.com/slovenia.

Middleton, Ian. "Three Santas in Slovenia—It's Good to Be a Slovenian Child at Christmas!" *Total Slovenia News*, November 21, 2018. https://www.total-slovenia-news.com/travel/2524-christmas-in-slovenia-with-three-santas.

Nature Parks of Slovenia. https://www.naravniparkislovenije.si/en.

Posedel, Andreja. "3 Inspiring Slovenian Sportswomen You Should Know About." Culture Trip, September 5, 2017. https://theculturetrip.com/europe/slovenia/articles/3-inspiring-slovenian-sportswomen-you-should-know-about.

Skledar, Stefan. "Austerity Measures Cause Conflict." *Eurofound*, October 4, 2012. https://www.eurofound.europa.eu/publications/article/2012/austerity-measures-cause-conflict.

Slovenia.si. http://www.slovenia.si.

UNESCO World Heritage Convention. "Slovenia." https://whc.unesco.org/en/statesparties/si.

United Nations Sustainable Development Solutions Network. "World Happiness Report 2018." https://worldhappiness.report.

INDEX

INDEX